KM/MW
KDON
KJOUR

DAY BY DAY

Day by Day

A Dose of My Own Hemlock

ROBIN DAY

WILLIAM KIMBER · LONDON

First published in 1975 by
WILLIAM KIMBER & CO. LIMITED
Godolphin House, 22a Queen Anne's Gate
London, SWiH 9AE

© Robin Day, 1961, 1963, 1970, 1975

ISBN 0 7183 0154 4

Made and printed in Great Britain by
The Garden City Press Limited
Letchworth, Hertfordshire SG6 1JS

*For
Kathy
and
Alexander*

Contents

List of Photographs

Illustrations in the Text

PART I

A Dose of My Own Hemlock

1. A Time for Self-questioning

Is not an interview with yourself a rather self-important way to mark your twentieth year on the television screen?
I cannot see why it is any more self-important for an interviewer to interview himself than for a writer to write about himself. It is certainly more unusual, and will probably be more critical.

But is not self-questioning, however critical, an egocentric process?
That would be so if the self-questioning had no other motive than interest in one's own self. That is not my motive here.

What is your motive?
It is to illuminate some of the problems of television in the light of my experience during these twenty years. I have become confused and anxious about the influence of television. My attitude to television has passed through different phases. At first it was one of uncritical excitement and enthusiasm.[1] Later my attitude became that of a busily involved professional, thinking less about the nature of the medium than about the next assignment, the next flight, the next interview, the next crisis to be covered. In more recent years my attitude to television and to my own part in it has become increasingly critical. I have become dissatisfied with television's coverage of issues. I have become disturbed about television's impact on events. I have begun to feel some disillusionment with that new branch of journalism which began to develop about twenty years ago—the television interview.

Hence this essay in critical self-questioning. You may recall a saying attributed to Socrates: 'The unexamined life is not worth living.'

Could you not achieve your aim by writing in the ordinary way instead of in question-and-answer form?
No doubt. But by inclination and experience I rather enjoy the

[1]See Part IV, pp. 143–224, reprinting chapters from *Television: A Personal Report* (1961).

Socratic method. I use the term in its colloquial sense—the conducting of argument and imparting of information by means of question and answer. So the object is a dialogue by self-examination.

Giving yourself a dose of your own hemlock?
I had not intended to follow Socrates that far. But who knows what the consequences may be?

But without others with whom to engage in genuine dialogue, should not your self-questioning be described as pseudo-Socratic?
Let's get off Socrates, though I would be very surprised if he did not frequently ask himself some very difficult questions. The dialogue will have a genuine basis because the questions will often arise from criticism made by others. There is no shortage of ammunition. My mind is a well-stocked arsenal of criticisms which have been levelled at me and my work by the public, the press and my professional colleagues.

My readers may also find that some of the more awkward questions would not have been put except in a self-interview, in which the interviewer can be said to have some degree of inside knowledge.

Before we leave Socrates, may I remind you that he was a philosopher and that his method was for a philosophical purpose? Do you have any such purpose in this question-and-answer dialogue?
To say 'yes' would sound intolerably pretentious, and I rather regret ever mentioning Socrates. To deny any such purpose, however, would be misleading. Philosophy in its conversational sense means a set of principles for the guidance of thought and action. In that limited sense, I have tried to work towards something like a philosophy for the use of television as a branch of journalism in a democracy like ours. My *Encounter* article[1] was an earlier effort in that direction.

A practitioner may feel too close to his work to be a philosopher of it. But practitioners of television should examine themselves and their experience, in order to seek a philosophy. Otherwise their professional thought and action will be increasingly governed not by principle or purpose, but by the mindless mechanics of the medium. The practitioner has a duty to ask himself not only how the medium *can* be used, but how the medium *ought* to be used.

[1]May 1970. See Part II, pp. 93–114.

But have not the television organizations, notably the BBC, built up their own corporate philosophies from long editorial experience and codified them into authoritative principles?

That is so. My thoughts are supplementary to those, and are merely the thoughts of one individual broadcaster. I am only a humble worker on the shop-floor of the great image factory. I do not speak with the voice of corporate authority. But the individual broadcaster has his own contribution, limited though that may be by his own professional experience, to make to the continuing public debate about television and its responsibilities. That debate has entered a critical period as the Annan Committee conducts its inquiry into the future of broadcasting in Britain.

Ideas about the responsibility of television are partly handed down by those who are constitutionally in ultimate control, and partly thrown up from below by those, like myself, who are directly involved in what appears on the screen. No one can work in the actual making of television programmes without examining and formulating his own ideas about this extraordinary means of communication.

That is what television is. It is a means of communication, not an end in itself. It is an instrument. Like nuclear explosive, television is one of man's most powerful and dangerous inventions. Man must think very seriously about how to use this instrument, lest it do him grievous harm.

TWENTY YEARS IN TELEVISION

Apart from the fact that twenty years is a nice round period over which to look back and take stock, what other significance is there in the period from 1955 to 1975?

The same twenty years have been the years of ITV's existence in competition with the BBC. I began my television career in Independent Television News when ITV started transmission on September 22nd 1955.[1] These two decades have been the period in which television in Britain grew up out of its infancy, and became firmly established as the main mass medium of information and entertainment.

So my twenty years have also been the years in which television

[1]See Part IV.

has become a part of everyday life, a part of journalism and a part of politics in a way it never was before 1955.

Because I entered television when ITV began, my start in television coincided with the enormous impetus which competition gave to the development of television as a new branch of journalism. This coincidence was also an opportunity which some of us seized with zest and determination. The result was that a major effect of ITV competition, and of the BBC's response to it, was to transform the atmosphere in television, to extend the boundaries of freedom and to begin making television's coverage of politics more worthy of a mature democracy.

Those of us whose television careers began in the mid-'fifties when competition began were lucky, but we deserve some credit for making use of the opportunity.

SWORDS, SHACKLES AND SHIELDS

What do you think your contribution was?
I would hope to be regarded as one of those who may be given credit for pioneering and developing a new concept of the broadcasters' impartiality and independence. After 1955, impartiality and independence came to be interpreted actively instead of passively. Fairness had to be more than a balance of opinions and the reporting of available facts. The duty to be fair had to be carried out actively, by inquiry into the facts, by revealing other facts. The duty of impartiality was seen as enhancing and not limiting the right to inquire. The acceptance of this interpretation has been one of the most important developments in the last twenty years. Having been a shackle, the impartiality principle became a sword.

Similarly with the idea of independence: the BBC had rightly prided itself on its independence. But it was a passive or negative independence —a shield against political interference. This was, and is, a tremendously important principle, envied and sometimes copied in other countries. But after the coming of ITV competition in 1955, the independence of broadcasters was interpreted more positively. There developed a new concept of independence—not merely independence from political interference but independence to inquire, to ascertain facts, to raise issues, to seek the truth. Having been a shield, the broadcasters' independence also became, like their impartiality, a sword in their hands.

. .

*Are you not putting it too dramatically with all this talk about swords and
shackles and shields? Are you allowing, perhaps, your nostalgic enthusiasm
for those early pioneering days to exaggerate the changes which occurred?*

It you don't like the metaphors of weaponry, I'm sorry. But if you
could spend a week watching the television of the early 'fifties (I am
talking about news and current affairs) you would realize that the
changes which began in the mid-'fifties have proved to be fundamental.
Television became a real rival to the newspapers not merely as
a speedier and more vivid communicator of happenings, but as a
maker of news, an investigator of issues, a presenter of argument, and a
projector of public personalities. Television became part of the political
process as never before. With its new vigour and freedom, television
not only *reported* public controversy but *created* it, in a way that rarely
happened in the heyday of radio, or in the early years of television.

The more vigorous and challenging did television journalism
become, the more did it come under attack for abuse of power, for
unfairness, for irresponsibility. This was a healthy reaction. It was also
a sign that television, because of its increasing journalistic vigour, had
arrived in the centre of democratic controversy. Television journalists
—executives, producers and reporters alike—had to hold their nerve,
and to keep sharp their swords of impartiality and independence.

WITHOUT FEAR OR FAVOUR

*Why do you say that the reaction against the new vigour of TV journalism
was 'healthy'? Were not some of the attacks aimed at curbing the activities
of reporters and interviewers like yourself?*

The reaction was a healthy one because it meant that television journalists were working under keen scrutiny. They had to be able to defend
their work as a justifiable use of their responsible position. An interviewer's questions had to be carefully and accurately phrased so as not
to lay the interviewer open to a charge of being offensive or of indulging his own prejudices. While not flinching from his duty as an
inquiring journalist, the interviewer had to act judiciously and courte-
ously. Needless to say, not everybody would agree that this difficult
combination was achieved. But the interviewer's duty was clear—if not
always carried out to every viewer's satisfaction—to ask the necessary
questions without fear or favour.

DAILY MIRROR

'We're trying to appease Wilson'

How does 'fear' come into it?

It is one thing to sit down in your office with a note-book and to compose a strongly-worded question which goes to the heart of an extremely important issue. It is quite another thing to put that question in those same words when you are face to face with the person being interviewed, not least if he happens to be the Prime Minister sitting in No. 10 Downing Street. In the presence of a statesman who bears the enormous burden of governing the country, a question which previously seemed fair and relevant may suddenly seem glib and unseemly. You are liable to feel how trivial is the interviewer's responsibility compared to that of a Cabinet Minister.

At such moments, the interviewer must stiffen his resolve and remember that out there, in millions of homes, are people who are angry or discontented or who want certain questions to be put. He must also remember that while due respect should be shown to those who hold high office, history reminds us that they often make errors of judgment and sometimes appalling blunders. They have also been known to speak with less than total frankness. If an interviewer loses his nerve and fails to put the crucial questions, he betrays the public who are relying on him.

Furthermore, in formulating and pressing his questions, he must fearlessly disregard the probability of politically-motivated attacks upon him for having asked questions which were 'hostile', i.e. which reflected an opposing point of view.

For a good many years now, anyone in the front line of television journalism has learned to expect that any major interview will be fiercely criticized, often on quite contradictory grounds. What is grossly impertinent to one critic may be nauseatingly sycophantic to another. What is praised as justifiably persistent in one newspaper may be condemned as hectoringly offensive in the next. At least one knows that both criticisms cannot be right.

Is there not a complacent tendency among broadcasters to assume that if a programme is attacked on contradictory grounds, or from both left and right, that therefore the programme must have been fair and worthy?

Such a tendency does exist. Broadcasters would be less than human if they did not sometimes defend themselves by pointing out how strongly they have been attacked on totally opposite grounds. That is a legitimate defensive reaction. It may be a useful tactic to keep the hounds at bay. But it should not be allowed to relieve the broadcaster from his duty of forming a professional judgment.

Very few pieces of work, in television journalism deserve no criticism. Some interviews are good but there is rarely one which could not have been done much better. The broadcaster should take note, without getting too smug, of those aspects of his work which appear to please or win praise. He should also take note, without getting too suicidal, that he is considered to be pompous, arrogant, offensive, truculent, bad-tempered, unfit for his job, a disgrace to the BBC, biased to the left, biased to the right and so on.

At the end of the day the broadcasters must honestly judge their work by those exacting standards which they must always try to uphold and which may not always be the prime concern of their critics: integrity, independence and excellence.

2. Myths and Misconceptions

Why did you say earlier that you feel some disillusionment with the television interview as a branch of journalism?

Because the television interview is rarely what it has been built up to seem. It has acquired a cliché image in peoples' minds which is wholly misleading. Television interviews have so often been described as 'ordeals' or 'gladiatorial combats' or 'grillings', that the public and the critics are too ready to assume that an interview is tough and searching when it may in fact have been soft and superficial. Thus may the public be often misled into thinking that the subject has been thoroughly handled.

Are you saying that the television interview has become a fraud upon the public?

That is what I am sometimes driven to feel, though 'fraud' is too strong a word, implying a deliberate intention to deceive. An interview may look tough and sound searching, but in reality may have only scraped the surface.

Do you feel that some of your own interviews are, in that sense, a fraud upon the public?

Some have not been quite what they may have seemed. After doing an inadequate interview I may read in the press that it was probing and penetrating. I may even be congratulated by executives to whom I am responsible. Yet I know perfectly well that the interview was superficial. Far from being too probing and too challenging, far too many TV interviews done by myself and others are neither probing nor challenging enough.

A television interview may be praised as 'penetrating' or attacked as 'a relentless inquisition' when it reality it is merely a series of rather obvious questions which cover only some of the facts. This may be a useful exercise, but rarely amounts to anything like 'an ordeal by cross-examination', 'interrogation' or 'inquisition'. Such descriptions have become part of the TV interview myth.

Why are there so many interviews in which the questioning is superficial? This is often due to lack of time. Although interviewers are encouraged to be persistent and thorough, they are frequently denied adequate time to achieve anything but that illusion of thoroughness which may mislead the viewer. But the inadequacy of an interview may also be the fault of the interviewer in failing to select his points properly, in lacking the ability to listen and follow up effectively, in having poorly briefed himself, or in being plain ignorant. For these faults, which are deplorably common, there can be no excuse.

THE 'OLD BAILEY' MISCONCEPTION

Inadequate though many interviews may be, the TV studio is often likened by critics to the Old Bailey. Interviewers are compared with prosecuting barristers dealing with a disreputable witness. Are there not some interviews which are done in that style?
It is very rare for a TV interview to be long enough or searching enough to bear any real resemblance to counsel's cross-examination of a witness in court. The analogy so often drawn between studio and courtroom is misconceived. The differences between the two situations are fundamental. A person being interviewed on television is not on oath. He has not sworn to tell the truth, the whole truth and nothing but the truth. In a TV studio there are no rules of evidence. There is no presiding judge to order that an interviewer's questions be answered (that would make a difference) or that a question should not be asked. A TV interview usually lasts only a few minutes which is scarcely adequate for a 'relentless cross-examination'.

But are not some TV interviews much longer than a few minutes? Your own interview with Lord Lambton, for example, was forty-five minutes, and seemed to most viewers a probing cross-examination.
I accept the point. But even if the interview is much longer than usual, it is nowhere near as long as a cross-examination in court which may go on for hours. It is true that Tony Lambton was questioned closely and at length. But though he chose to give some sensationally frank answers

to pointed and personal questions, he was entirely free not to do so. There were, moreover, many questions which I did not ask, which might have been asked by counsel in court, whose responsibility would not be that of a journalist, but that of a lawyer with a duty to the court and to his client, and who would not be getting TV time-signals.

A barrister can go over a point again and again, taking his time, leading the witness into a carefully prepared trap. Unlike counsel in court the TV interviewer has no right to have his questions answered specifically or at all. His questions can easily be brushed aside by an answer which deals with something quite different in the knowledge that the interviewer may have neither time nor persistence to press the question.

But is it not a fact, whether you agree with the analogy or not, that to many viewers, some TV interviews look and sound like a hostile cross-examination in court?

That may be so, but to anyone familiar with the courts the comparison is nonsense. Judges and barristers have often complained to me about the ineffectuality of an interview which lay viewers or press critics have considered 'searching' or 'relentless'. On one occasion after I had interviewed an eminent politician well-known for his evasive skill, I was asked: 'Next time you interview that slippery Mr X, why don't you question him like this: "Mr X, did you hear my question? Mr X, did you understand my question? Mr X, will you now answer my question?"' I explained that there could be only one interview in which I would ever be tempted to employ such a technique—my last.

Another suggestion once made to me by a veteran exponent of the forensic art will show that the worlds of the legal cross-examiner and the TV interviewer are far apart. I invited suggestions for an opening question to be used in an interview with a certain leading politician. The lawyer thought for a moment and replied: 'Start by asking him this: Does the word *shame* mean anything to you?'

This is the kind of question associated with some of the flamboyant court-room cross-examiners of the past. After due consideration I came to the conclusion that there were better ways of starting the interview.

What a pity.
I detect a sense of mischief in you.

Though the court-room analogy may be wrong, would you deal with the criticism made by quite fair-minded people that sometimes the interviewer seems to be treating a public man as if he were a crook?

It is not an interviewer's job to imply any such thing. His job is to ask fair and relevant questions and to leave the viewer to draw his own conclusions. It is an abuse of an interviewer's position if his questioning is so conducted as to suggest that the man is a crook or a liar, unless there is clear evidence to support such questioning. It will not be difficult to recall a recent and bizarre case, involving a political figure with whom any interview would have had to include questions based on facts which clearly reflected on his integrity.

An answer may be given which appears to be flatly contrary to or inconsistent with known facts. It is then the interviewer's duty to put a follow-up question (not an accusation) based on the known facts. In politics, however, truth is many-sided. The interviewee will offer his own interpretation of 'the known facts'. The interviewer must then judge whether that interpretation should be probed further, either because his own knowledge tells him that this is clearly necessary or because his instinct tells him that the viewers, or a substantial section of them, may be less than satisfied with the answers.

To take a more common situation, the interviewee may attempt to dismiss the points raised in an evasive and obviously unconvincing manner. It is then perfectly justifiable for an interviewer to pursue the line of questioning with persistence. There was one particular occasion with a leading politician at a Party Conference. I was being so persistent that even I began to feel that the point had been flogged too hard. Immediately after the interview ended and we were off the air, the politician leant over to speak to me. I thought he was going to complain. Instead, to my astonishment, he whispered, 'Your questions were perfectly justified. My position is *totally indefensible*.' He spoke those last two words with bitter emphasis. Yet I am sure that some viewers, particularly of that politician's party, felt that he had been subjected to a repetitious, unfair and even insulting cross-examination.

DUTY AND DISCIPLINE

Is it not rather presumptuous to speak of the public relying on an interviewer to ask certain questions? Are you not assuming too much importance for yourself?

It is not a question of assuming or presuming anything. Unless the interviewer works on the principle that he has a duty to those watching and that they are entitled to have critical questions put, he is working with no sense of purpose except to indulge his own curiosity and cleverness. For the interviewer to feel a duty to the public is not to assume exaggerated importance. It is a vital way by which the interviewer must continually discipline himself to concentrate on questions which matter for people who are watching. He must resist the temptation to ask questions which are too clever by half. He must not get embroiled in personal altercation if the interviewee (as sometimes happens) chooses to answer an awkward question by a personal jibe at the interviewer.

Have you always managed to discipline yourself in this way?

If you press me: No. But whenever I allow myself to be stung into some retort the effect on the interview is always bad. Despite the momentary satisfaction of defending myself, this has usually distracted from the purpose of the interview, which is to inform the public about an important issue. A personal clash of this kind, however brief, lays the interviewer open to the charge of setting himself up as a public duellist, which is not what he is paid to be. The interviewer must always remember that a politician, especially one who is under attack, is fully entitled to defend himself, and to hit back at an interrogator. Indeed I am surprised that more politicians do not hit back, particularly at questioners who mistake hectoring for persistence and who have not done their homework.

But don't the viewers enjoy those rare moments—when an interview is suddenly enlivened by a flash of personal sword-play between interviewer and interviewee?

Get thee behind me Satan. It is one of television's constant temptations to provoke some sort of conflict or 'scene' which may amuse or excite the viewer. But for every viewer who may be amused or excited, there are others who may be infuriated when a subject which deeply concerns them is cheapened by knockabout remarks. That again is why it is so important for an interviewer to think first about his duty to the public.

When an interviewer has a personal jibe thrown at him he should take it in his stride, keep his temper and show his sense of humour.

He can take comfort from the knowledge that when an interviewee feels obliged to answer by resorting to a personal jibe this probably means the question was a pertinent one.

But surely there are some occasions when the interviewer should defend himself?

Yes, of course there are. If the interviewer, for example, is accused of asking an unfair, improper or irrelevant question, he is fully entitled to defend his right to ask it, if the point is important. But he should avoid doing so by argumentative assertions or counter-attack. He should first ask why the question was unfair or improper. Depending on the answer, he must then use his discretion as to whether he should defend the question to which objection was taken. In doing so, he should confine himself to a brief justification of his question in a way which will not provoke further attack (e.g. '. . . But this matter has been raised by the Opposition and was the subject of a critical resolution at your own Party Conference'). He should then persist with the question. This may not be easy and will call for strong self-control, especially if the atmosphere of the interview is exciting and the occasion is dramatic—as at certain moments in a General Election campaign.

'DON'T GET TOUCHY ABOUT IT, ROBIN'

Was there not just such a moment in one of your interviews with Mr Wilson in the General Election of February 1974?

You have an embarrassingly good memory. Yes. It was in an interview 'down the line' from London with Mr Wilson who was in the Norwich studio. The question which caused the trouble was based on one of the points which Mr Heath, then Prime Minister, had been making: 'Do you think the miners are justified in continuing their strike?' Mr Wilson's reply was that the nation was tired of such questions put by Mr Heath and 'now peddled by you'. I felt it right to object to the word 'peddled' because I was merely doing the impartial journalist's job of inviting comment on an opponent's 'challenge', as with one of Mr Wilson's challenges to Mr Heath. My mistake was, apparently, to seem too irritated about it. Anyway Mr Wilson immediately came back: 'Don't get so sensitive. You're in politics. Don't behave like a child about it. Don't get touchy about it, Robin.'

At this point I could clearly see in my mind the next morning's headlines—'Wilson in clash with Robin Day', which would merely create bad blood. So I avoided any altercation and repeated the same question, but in a different way to which Mr Wilson made no objection. I don't think for a moment that Mr Wilson was accusing me of unfairness or bias. In objecting to the question he was simply giving vent to his annoyance with a point which Mr Heath had kept raising. David Butler in his book on the February 1974 election records that there was irritation at Labour's press conference towards journalists who persisted in 'retailing' this point of Mr Heath's to Mr Wilson and others. So I did not take what Mr Wilson said as a personal attack on me. I objected at the time, because of the need to let the public know that the question was not put with bias, but as part of a reporter's duty. If I sounded 'touchy', that was an error which gave Mr Wilson an opportunity which he was quite entitled to seize. There was no trouble afterwards and no repercussions that I heard of.

I should perhaps mention that 'down the line' interviews seem to carry a greater risk of a 'row' occurring than when interviewer and interviewee are sitting together at a table after a chat and a drink. When the interviewee is in a different studio in another part of the country there is a remoteness in the occasion, added to which the interviewee may have had to wait alone, tired after a heavy day's campaigning, for an irritatingly long time for the interview to be done. I have no evidence that any of these factors applied in the case of that interview with Mr Wilson in Norwich—but I would be surprised if they were not part of the explanation for his uncharacteristic objection to one of my questions.

Uncharacteristic?

Yes, because Mr Wilson is an old parliamentary hand and a masterly performer on television. I cannot recall any other occasion in which he has taken exception, during or after an interview, to any question of mine, however critical. And I am sure he did not think this question was unfair. In fact after interviews he has sometimes ticked me off for having failed to put a good supplementary question which might have caused him difficulty.

The incident, by the way, is a reminder of what is the most lamentable gap in all General Election television: the absence of any debate between party leaders facing each other across a table. Such a debate

'Yes, Mr Day, I'm still Prime Minister because the Tory Party was so busy fighting its leadership elections every year, that it forgot all about the General Elections . . .'

DAILY EXPRESS

would be given generous time and would attract a huge audience. Interviews, however well conducted, in which one leader's points have to be put, if not peddled, to the other are no substitute; nor are the party election broadcasts, which are delivered in isolation on different nights.

The mass-audience should be able to see reasoned argument, at length and in juxtaposition, between those who aspire to lead, or to continue leading, the nation. It is to be hoped that the broadcasting authorities will not be inhibited about strongly urging (and with public invitations so that the electorate may know who has vetoed the idea) that debates between party leaders should become a central feature of General Election broadcasting.

3. 'Panorama' and the BBC

May we turn to some of the professional arguments and problems which have arisen in your career as a TV journalist? Take Panorama, *of which you ceased to be anchorman in January 1972: had you not been involved in arguments about how that programme should be run?*

Yes: but arguments about how *Panorama* should be run had gone on for many years. Whoever was anchorman, whoever was editor, whoever were the reporters, there were arguments about the programme's function and purpose and how it should be best achieved. Such arguments were one reason why *Panorama* was often such a fine programme. The history of good broadcasting is the history of creative conflict between lively strong-minded people who would not be in their jobs unless they had the ability and the desire to fight for the best result.

One of my consistent arguments for several years had been that *Panorama* was in danger of losing its impact and interest if it became too much of a single-subject film documentary programme. This did not mean I was urging a return to the 'fifties format of several items which were often too short and trivial. I argued for a balance between topicality and prolonged documentary treatment, between studio and film, between talk and pictures—a balance which would have also retained the value of the anchorman's role. I felt that the role of anchorman should not be reduced to that of an announcer with a couple of thirty-second links. How well I remember Richard Dimbleby saying the same thing after a *Panorama* in which he had been given virtually nothing to do.

May not this attitude have given the impression that you wanted Panorama *to be a 'vehicle for Robin Day'?*

There could be no grounds for such an impression. I had never suggested any such thing. I had spent twelve years as a member of the *Panorama* team and believed that one of its great strengths lay in the different styles of its reporters. I objected to the deliberate erosion of the anchorman's position because I believed it to be an important factor in the appeal, authority and continuity of the programme.

Can you deny that there was considerable self-interest in that view?
Obviously no one likes to feel their capacities are being wasted. But my
defence against the charge of self-interest is that I held exactly the same
view when Richard Dimbleby was anchorman. I held the same view
when Alastair Burnet (for whom I have the highest regard and admira-
tion) succeeded me as anchorman until he became editor of the *Daily
Express*. I could not understand the point of hiring such a strong and
brilliant personality as Burnet without giving him more to do in his
role as anchorman.

EXIT DAY

What was the reason for your ceasing to be the anchorman of Panorama *in
January 1972, after more than twelve years with that programme, five as
anchorman?*
The immediate reason was simply that I was not offered a new contract
as the *Panorama* anchorman. Rather than accept a brief and temporary
extension I went when the old contract expired.

*Was not the decision to discontinue your position as anchorman one which
the BBC was perfectly entitled to take, whether you liked it or not?*
Oh certainly. The BBC or any other television organization has the
right and the duty to take such decisions if they are judged to be
desirable. Those who 'appear' have no God-given right to do so. Someone in my position, however well-known and experienced he may be,
must always understand that his career is entirely at the mercy of those
who have the power at any time to decide the content of programmes.
No less a person than the great Richard Dimbleby often warned me of
this very danger.

I vividly recall Richard's reply when I once suggested that he of all
people had a rocksafe position in television: 'My dear boy, don't you
believe it for a moment. There is always liable to be someone who
wants a new face, or who thinks your image is wrong, or who wants to
demonstrate that he has the power.' He would continually urge me to
'have other irons in the fire'.

Richard Dimbleby knew what he was talking about. It is no secret
that two *Panorama* Editors wanted to remove him from the role of
Panorama anchorman.

ARGUMENTS ABOUT *PANORAMA*

Was your part in the arguments about how Panorama *should be run the underlying reason which led to your departure from the position of anchorman?*

That may well have been one reason but I think there was a mixture of reasons. I honestly do not know for certain what the deciding factor was. To speculate would put me in danger of imputing motives, without having first-hand evidence.

Perhaps the best available evidence as to thinking in the BBC at that time is to be found in the explanations given by newspaper journalists who made their own inquiries. Their impressions, independently gained from off-the-record discussion with BBC people, may be of greater and more objective value than any speculation by me. An *Observer* profile, which appeared the week after I left *Panorama*, reported that I had made enemies among television people who resented my independence. 'There is opposition to him,' recorded the *Observer*, 'among some of the new young BBC producers who are trying to re-vamp *Panorama*, only to be blocked, it is said, by the patriarchial presence of Day.' The *Observer* noted that I had been featured less and less prominently on *Panorama*.

In the *Sunday Telegraph*, Mr Ivan Rowan concluded that some of the tensions 'had their source in the strength of Day's views on how the programme should be handled, and his inexhaustible advocacy of them, which wearied and exasperated many executives: "No case is ever closed with Robin until it's gone to the House of Lords." '

'TALKING HEADS AND MOVING PICTURES'

Miss Polly Toynbee recorded the results of her researches for the *Observer* magazine. According to her conclusion, my presence on *Panorama* 'seemed to the young producers an insurmountable obstacle'. Miss Toynbee's inquiries produced the following version of what the difficulties were about:

'There was a real and serious conflict between Day and the Young Turks of the BBC. It was about what should be shown on the screen, and it became known as the Talking Heads school versus the Moving Pictures school. Day, champion of Talking Heads, believes that much of politics is concerned with complex ideas and policies that can only be adequately presented through serious discussion. Pictures are often distracting; and worse, the need to show interesting pictures often means that producers trivialise the content in order to twist the subject round to make it viewable. The Moving Pictures faction argues that the public can't listen to or understand two establishment upper middle-class figures fencing with words in a way that bears no relation to the way people actually live. And they add with a savage side swipe, Robin Day promotes the Talking Head argument only because it keeps his own talking head on the screen.'[1]

Is that account fair?

It's a fair account of how some people saw my position. But any idea that I was or am against 'Moving Pictures' was a ludicrous distortion of my attitude. As a television reporter, I have made a vast number of films (often in the dual capacity of reporter-producer) with great professional enthusiasm. I was one of the first people who worked with 16mm sound camera teams to use film for vivid natural news reporting.[2] The Suez invasion was one of the occasions when this was first successfully done.

I have always argued that a good topical news-magazine needs a mix of both elements: 'live' studio argument, and reports on film.

It is perfectly true that the 'live' interview and the 'live' debate have come to acquire a special appeal for me. This is not because it keeps my 'talking head' on the screen—which is a rather cheap suggestion reflecting only on those who made it—but for very simple professional reasons. The first is that responsibility for a film is usually divided among several people—cameraman, film editor, producer, programme editor—in addition to the reporter. For a 'live' programme, the reporter as interviewer or chairman is briefed by his Editor and is then entrusted with the responsibility of conducting the programme with all the problems which that involves. A film is a committee product. Though a studio programme also requires a team, the interviewer or chairman has the responsibility of being, to a very considerable extent, in charge during transmission. None of this means that I am against film, which

[1]The *Observer* magazine, July 14, 1974.
[2]See Part IV.

is obviously an indispensable part of television journalism, particularly in a programme like *Panorama*. If the 'Young Turks' told Polly Toynbee that I was against 'moving pictures', they must have been so young as to have no recollection of the innumerable films made by me which are in the *Panorama* archives—films made all over the world, in America, Europe, Africa, Russia, Cuba, South East Asia, Australia, and here at home.

'BLOODY GOOD PICTURES' ARE NOT ENOUGH

There is another reason why, in the last few years, I have been particularly interested in 'live' interviews and discussion. I have come to feel very strongly that television, which has such an enormous power to project violence and unreason, should do more to present reasoned and civilized argument which is the basis of our democratic system. The electronic journalism of television must do much more than transmit 'bloody good pictures'.

Are you suggesting that there are people in television who are against 'reasoned argument' or the democratic system?
There have been times when I have felt that my passionate belief in parliamentary democracy and fair debate was regarded in some television circles as a rather old-fashioned 'establishment' attitude. I have never shared the trendy cynical disillusionment with parliamentary politics which became part of the atmosphere in television no less than outside it. A whiff of that atmosphere can be detected in Polly Toynbee's piece which I've just quoted, where she refers to the view that my kind of political interview consists merely of establishment figures 'fencing' with words which the public 'can't understand', Such a comment, of course, could equally be made, and has been made, about Parliament itself. It is contemptuous not only of parliamentary debate, but of the 'public'. The public may not feel respect for some politicians, or for certain actions of Parliament, but they do not despise their parliamentary system.

During the last twenty years I have had literally thousands of letters and comments which show that despite the limitations I have admitted, television interviews with leading parliamentarians, conducted on a serious level, are well understood and widely appreciated, even among those whom some media people patronizingly call real people.

I have never hesitated to defend these unfashionable views, which have led to my being regarded in some quarters as a symbol of 'institutional politics'. This was a phrase of abuse much in vogue at one time. There was an extraordinary article in the BBC's own *Radio Times*[1] about five years ago which actually referred to 'allegations' that I had 'an old-fashioned attachment to government by debate'. Note the world 'allegations', clearly implying that what I was attached to was something reprehensible. What was I supposed to have an attachment to? Government by computer? Government by petrol-bomb? Government by mob? Government by jack-boot?

OLD REPORTERS AND YOUNG PRODUCERS

Will you not admit that in the period leading up to your departure from Panorama *there was considerable agreement with your own reported comment that you were 'rather old hat'?*
Irony is apt to boomerang heavily. Certainly, anyone who has been on television as long as I have must face the fact, and face it with a sense of humour, that he is not exactly a fresh new face. But there was more to it than merely being 'old hat' in the sense of having been around a long time.

Polly Toynbee, after her inquiries in the television world, summed it up with brutal simplicity in her *Observer* magazine article:

'As Robin Day has got older, producers have got younger, and clashes were almost inevitable.'

Can you deny the truth in that?
I am not exempt from the laws of nature. I cannot deny that I have got older. Indeed I must confess that this year, 1975, I am for the first time older than one of the two main national party leaders—Mrs Margaret Thatcher.

With regard to producers and executives, as each new generation comes into programme-making work it is true that the gap in years

[1]*Radio Times* issue dated February 22nd 1970.

between their age-group and mine is larger. But I would deny any implication that as I have got older I have had endless quarrels with young producers. That is absolute rubbish. In the vast majority of cases, and increasingly so in recent years, I happen to have got on very well with young producers. One reason is that they like working in an atmosphere of laughter, which for some reason I am apt to generate around me. They are pleasantly surprised to find I am less unenjoyable to work with than some of the hospitality-room gossip has led them to believe.

Has there been no basis at all for such gossip?
Gossip in the hot-house of television is an even more intense activity than in a school or a newspaper office. It surpasses in malice even the gossip of Westminster. Gossip feeds on itself. An isolated incident is picked up, passed on, embroidered and made to sound typical. A remark made in the fun of argument, in the tension of work, is repeated out of context. An exacting insistence on trying to achieve high standards can easily be labelled 'difficult to work with'. There is always some ill-concealed jealousy of the well-known and relatively well-paid figure who appears 'in vision' on the screen.

PERSONAL FAULTS

Are you implying that you have no personal faults—faults of personality— which can create difficulties?
Everybody has faults. My television colleagues have faults. I have my share.

What are yours?
I find myself trapped into a very awkward position. I would find it difficult, not to say embarrassing, to make a truthful list. After all, what I may consider a virtue may appear as a fault to someone else, and vice versa. My sense of objectivity is strong, but not really ruthless enough for such intimate self-analysis.

Whose idea was it to conduct this self-interview in the first place?
I'm beginning to regret it. But to attempt a reasonably honest answer, I would plead that my only relevant faults were the faults which a

charitably-minded person might say were the natural accompaniment of my better qualities. For example, the obstinacy which goes with strong convictions, the vehemence which can arise out of enthusiasm, the impatience which goes with an experienced professional sense of what seems obvious, the causticity of criticism which stems from exacting professional standards. And I should perhaps add, a tendency to genial but not always appreciated abuse which comes with a boisterous love of humour in argument.

I would have thought that such personality traits were common enough in any field of creative activity where ideas and issues are involved.

Do you still feel yourself regarded in television as a symbol of old-fashioned 'establishment' ideas on parliament, democracy and debate?

Not in such a hostile sense as previously. I may be wrong, but I feel there has been a rethinking, especially among the younger generation, of what television's responsibilities are. This reaction has been brought about by growing awareness of the dangers of violence, disruption and unreason in our society. There has been a corresponding reaction against the kind of current affairs television which depends for its appeal on noisy and incoherent emotionalism rather than on reasonable argument. People got bored with the Frost-style shout-in. Others were more than bored. They were concerned that television was too often lending its power to the irresponsible trivialization of important issues.

TV'S GENERATION GAP

Why is there so big a generation gap between the older reporters and the young producers in current affairs television?

This is because the older reporters have remained in the same position, but with increasing experience, ever since they entered television when they were younger—perhaps ten or twenty years ago. But the producer moves up the executive ladder. He starts as a trainee or a production assistant, becomes an assistant producer, then a producer, an assistant Editor and then perhaps an Editor. If he is picked out for executive promotion he becomes Head of a Department, a Controller and so on up the hierarchy. So there is a continual influx of new young people to become producers at the programme-making level.

Your veteran reporter may find himself working under an Editor with great power over his professional career, whom he recalls working with as a very green production assistant, anxious to learn and make progress, and not unwilling for the reporter to put in a word on his behalf to those in charge.

Let me emphasize that I am not the only TV journalist who has got older as the producers have got younger. Nor am I the only TV journalist who has experienced the problems this can create. I was one of that original generation of television journalists, an entirely new breed of broadcaster, who began their work on the screen in the 'fifties. Because of the war and because there had been very few opportunities in television until the 'fifties, they did not start in television until they were about ten or fifteen years older than the age at which today's entrants begin. They had become established and experienced professionals by the end of the 'sixties. This was the very period when television's expansion was bringing in a whole new generation of young producers and executives-to-be, many of them straight from the universities.

Do you think you will survive the 'seventies, whose intake will be an even younger generation—some twenty years your junior in experience and thirty years your junior in age?

Who knows? I shall take what comes, if I'm still around. But the 'seventies do not seem to have brought in the same flood of young recruits which we saw in the expansion—explosion is perhaps the word —of television in the 'sixties. The young graduates of the 'seventies have not spent their formative years in quite such a revolutionary atmosphere of university upheaval and challenge to authority as that which flared up in the late 'sixties. We shall see. But it would be a good idea if there could be more serious consideration of this sensitive and relatively new problem—the relationship between the experienced 'contributor' and the less experienced producer-executive.

TV'S PROFESSIONAL APARTHEID

After twenty years of development in television journalism there is still a far too rigid apartheid between the editorial executive and the journalist-contributor, between the producer and the 'performer' (a contemptuous and misleading description which suggests he is an actor or a circus animal).

This apartheid is a hangover from an earlier era in broadcasting when regular current affairs broadcasters were few, and regarded as gifted amateurs who were privileged to enjoy the patronage of the BBC's permanent staff who trained and produced them. I am not complaining about the BBC's right and duty of editorial control. That is fundamental and must be upheld. But there is no good reason why the experienced professional who 'appears' should not, in suitable cases, be given more responsibility in editorial decisions and programme policy.

Do you not make such a contribution?
Only to a particular item or programme in which I happen to be personally involved, and subject to the decisions of whoever is editing it. I am an 'outside' contributor. I am completely outside the Corporation's machinery of programme planning, policy discussions, programme review boards, etc. I have no knowledge of what is being decided and planned or why, unless somebody happens to tell me. I have, it is true, put up personal suggestions of my own. There is nothing to stop me doing that by letter or telephone. But though one can put up programmes ideas it is difficult to contribute constructively and intelligently if you are outside the system, and have no direct knowledge of the thinking inside. I think this apartheid could be broken down to some extent with considerable benefit to the Corporation. One result would be a much better use of some of the experience which is available, especially in the political field.

TOO BIG FOR HIS BOOTS?

Was it your interest in having more than a contributing performer's responsibility which in 1970 led you to apply for the Director-Generalship of the ITA (as it was then called)?
At that time, though I was still anchorman of *Panorama*, I was beginning to wonder (being then in my late forties) what I would be doing in my fifties. The advertisement for the ITA post caught my attention and made me think. Here was a case, rare in Britain, of an important public position being advertised for open competition instead of being filled by the usual behind-the-scenes method. Why

not give the selectors—the Members of the Authority—the opportunity to consider me? Judging from the advertisement, I appeared to have some, at least, of the specified qualifications. There was nothing to lose, except that some people in the BBC might think I was getting too big for my boots.

But did you think you had any serious chance of being appointed?
No. I was always convinced that the Authority would choose an uncontroversial figure with an administrative background. But I did feel, correctly as it turned out, that I had a good chance of being seriously considered and of reaching the final short list. I thought that this would not do me any harm, and might even be taken as a signal that I was worth considering for some other position of responsibility.

In the BBC?
Not necessarily.

But in broadcasting?
Not necessarily.

So you were flying a kite?
I would not put it quite like that. The notion that my application, though likely to fail, might conceivably lead to some other opportunity was only an afterthought. I was very serious in making the application and took enormous pains over it. But I suppose I was also making a gesture against a prevailing notion that those who happen to have acquired a reputation as 'communicators' or 'personalities' are thereby disqualified from holding a responsible position.

4. The Interviewer's Responsibility

Would you answer a question which must be in many people's minds: Do you not have a great deal of power and responsibility in your present job on the screen, indeed some would say too much?

That is a complicated question. I accept that a television journalist in my position, particularly when he interviews political leaders on important issues, has considerable responsibility. The nature and limits of that responsibility are misunderstood, and must be explained. If a programme is 'live' or recorded for unedited use shortly afterwards, the interviewer is responsible to his Editor for the fair and proper conduct of the interview. He will have consulted with his Editor in advance, though time and programme pressures may not always make a detailed discussion possible. That is why the interviewer must be someone whose professional knowledge and judgment can be completely trusted by his Editor in an unscripted programme.

So the interviewer goes into his assignment with an editorial brief, either express or understood, sometimes particular, sometimes general. But no matter how detailed the Editor's instructions or suggestions may be, he has to rely on the interviewer to cope with what may arise once the interview has started. That is where the interviewer's responsibility lies. The ultimate responsibility for the programme is that of the Corporation or ITV company which may be putting it out. But during transmission or recording, the interviewer is entrusted to exercise the *momentary* responsibility, on behalf of those who hold the *ultimate* responsibility.

It has to be exercised in a difficult combination of circumstances which have no parallel in journalism: the unscripted dialogue, the drama of the occasion, the gravity of the subject, the importance of the interviewee's position, the political feeling and pressures which may surround the occasion, the split-second timing, the instantaneous reactions which may be necessary, the need for careful phrasing of questions and a balanced selection of points, the consequences of an ill-judged phrase or a verbal slip, and above all the simultaneous awareness of a huge mass audience, daunting not only for its size but for the fact that it includes many critical viewers who may be expert on the subject, dons and diplomats, housewives (oh yes, they are experts) and company directors, trade unionists and Cabinet Ministers.

There is another aspect of the interviewer's responsibility which is unique in journalism. Although he works under editorial direction, a television interviewer's unscripted words, when he is 'live' on the air, go at once to the audience without any editorial or legal 'filter'. (There is of course a cut-off switch for extreme emergencies but that is not relevant to normal conditions.) Admittedly the newspaper journalist has to work at great pressure, but he at least has the satisfaction of knowing that others—sub-editors, lawyers, the Editor—will improve it, check it, authorize it, before it is published to the world. There is no such protection for the television journalist when he is working 'live'. So his responsibility, not only for the accuracy and fairness of his material, but for the avoidance of libel and contempt of court, is direct, personal and immediate.

That is the nature of the responsibility which may be entrusted to the television journalist. It includes a duty to make instant and well-judged decisions which no one else can make for him at the moment he has to make them—what Mr Donald Tyerman has called 'the autonomy of the instant voice.'

What safeguard is there to ensure that the interviewer does not do his job incompetently or improperly?
The obvious and ultimate safeguard is that he will not be employed in similar interviews again if he abuses his position or shows himself to be incompetent. If of course the programme is recorded it may be possible not to transmit it if it is a very bad one; but this may sometimes be impracticable.

TOO MUCH POWER?

But the point of the original question was whether an interviewer like yourself has too much power?
The interviewer's power is defined by the extent of the responsibility just explained. His power lies in his choice and phrasing of questions, what to ask, when to persist, when to move on, but that power must

be exercised within the terms of the responsibility entrusted to him by his Editor. That is to say, the interviewer's choice of questions must be in line with the express or understood instructions of his Editor, and with the general duty of accuracy and impartiality imposed on his organization. The interviewer does *not* have the power to indulge his own prejudices and opinions. If he does, he is abusing his responsibility, or has been wrongly encouraged by his Editor to conduct a biased or prejudiced interview.

But do not interviewers frequently appear to be indulging their own views or prejudices?

That is how it may often look. But everyone should remember that the interviewer, in the interests of fairness, has a duty to put critical questions which reflect views opposed to those of the interviewee. The trouble is that viewers who have strong political sympathies will regard critical questions to a politician they support as hostile and biased, whereas equally critical questions to someone they oppose will be regarded as right and proper, or far too deferential.

If I may return to the question of the interviewer's alleged power, it is important to emphasize the power which he does *not* have. If Mr Wedgwood Benn said (as reported[1]) that 'It is people like Robin Day . . . who today decide what we hear and who we see', I do not understand what he meant. The interviewer does not have the power to arrange the programme, or to invite the interviewee. He does not have the power, contrary to a widespread misconception, to compel anyone to appear on television to be interviewed. There is no such thing as a Robin Day *subpoena*. He does not have power to decide the length of the programme or the length of the interview. He does not have the power to appoint or control the Editor or producer.

The interviewer's power lies almost entirely in his handling of the interview, but subject to the restraints and editorial guidelines which I have explained. Otherwise his power lies only in his right to put forward ideas for programme content and his ability to get those ideas accepted. That aspect of his power will depend of course on the merit of his ideas, his experience, his persuasive skill and his relationship with his Editor.

[1] *Evening Standard*, March 4th 1975.

*Would you deal with the criticism that the interviewer has too much power
for 'one non-elected individual', particularly when he interviews the Prime
Minister at a time of national crisis?*

I have explained the limits of his power. To refer to him as 'one non-
elected individual' is true, but misleading. In the first place he is not
operating as a free-wheeling individual. He is working as part of a
programme team, under the direction of an Editor, and on behalf of an
organization such as the BBC or ITN. Most importantly he is working
under a known set of editorial rules which preclude, or should
preclude, any improper individual enterprise on his part.

As to his being 'non-elected', no interviewer that I know of has ever
claimed to be elected. But the interviewer is employed by, and can be
dismissed by, an organization which is constitutionally established by
the democratic will of Parliament to provide television and radio
services. The organizations which employ the interviewers are under
the broad control of independent people (the BBC Governors and the
Members of the IBA) who are appointed by the democratically elected
Government of the day.

Thus it will be seen that though the television interviewer is non-
elected, his professional rights and duties derive not from his own
self-importance or lust for power but from a constitutional authority
to broadcast which is democratically granted. Those who exercise that
authority appoint him, if they so choose, to do a particular job. In
angry letters to the press, TV interviewers are often described as 'self-
appointed'. Whatever else they may be, they are certainly not that.

*But is there anything in the constitutional basis of broadcasting which says
that a Prime Minister is answerable to Robin Day or any other interviewer?*

Of course not. Nor is any Prime Minister so answerable. He does not
have to appear unless he wishes to. He can reject (which often happens)
or accept any invitation to be interviewed on television. Even if he
accepts, he can easily avoid giving a specific answer to a particular
question. In the House of Commons, to which a Prime Minister is
answerable, a reply may be demanded of him in a way that would not
be tolerated on television. It should also be remembered that an interviewer's function is not to put questions as an individual speaking from
his own point of view, but as a journalist inquiring on behalf of others
and reflecting critical or opposing views.

USURPER OF PARLIAMENT?

That may be all right in theory, but has not the TV interview, with its mass audience and its probing questions, become a disproportionately important event which can seem to usurp the function of Parliament as the prime forum of political questioning and debate?

That has always been one of my arguments[1] for having the cameras in the Commons. The televising of Parliament will enable us to see our political leaders questioned by our elected representatives. Interviews by 'non-elected' interviewers would then cease to have the importance, real or imaginary, which they may now have. To see Harold Wilson questioned by Margaret Thatcher, instead of Harold Wilson questioned by Robin Day, would in my respectful submission, be a step forward in democratic communication. So my belief in televising parliament can hardly be said to be motivated by self-interest. Not that I am dedicated to abolishing the interviewer's job entirely. Something tells me there would still be times when I could continue to perform my function as a humble seeker after truth—for instance, when Parliament is not sitting, and during General Election campaigns when there are quite a few useful questions to be asked.

Incidentally, though I've always understood the objections to the TV interviewer's position, we should not get it out of perspective. Parliamentarians have derived great advantages from the television interview. Mr Jo Grimond has pointed out that when MPs are interviewed by the press it is the journalist who decides what should be used. But television, he says, gives them the chance to appear in their own image and to say what they have to say. According to Mr Grimond 'If it wasn't for TV and Radio they could be destroyed by the press and some of them have been virtually destroyed by the press'.

In fairness to newspapermen, I should mention that filmed and recorded interviews can also be edited by the broadcasters, and even a 'live' appearance can be abruptly interrupted or cut short. But Mr Grimond's point has much force and should be remembered.

According to the *Times* report, Mr Grimond was so emphatic about the benefits of the broadcast interview that he went on to make a moving suggestion: 'Politicians should fall down on their knees and

[1]See Part III, p. 117.

'Well, we've finally found someone from inside Number Ten who will talk to us . . .'

DAILY MIRROR

thank the Lord for television and radio.' Obviously there is a gap in the Book of Common Prayer which Parliament should seek to fill. Something quite simple such as: 'We thank thee O Lord, who art the author and giver of all good things, for this the medium provided by thy bounty.' There could be a brief confessional addition for use during General Election campaigns: 'We have left unsaid those things which we ought to have said, and we have said those things we ought not to have said.'

Why not an annual service of thanksgiving at St Margaret's Westminster, perhaps?
That might be overdoing it.

'TWENTY YEARS ON A TIGHTROPE'

One thing which may puzzle some people: if the power of a television interviewer is really subject to all the restraints and limits which you have mentioned, and if he does not operate as a 'free-wheeling individual', how is it that you have managed to acquire what is said to be such a powerful screen image as an individual personality?
Because I have never abused the responsibility entrusted to me, nor exceeded the powers which are delegated to an interviewer. Never—despite whatever unsolicited 'screen image' I may be lumbered with. No one has ever asked me to assume a false personality or to be a non-entity. All they have demanded is that I do my job according to certain standards of impartiality, accuracy, taste, etc. Which I have done. If I had failed in this respect, I would not have lasted twenty years in an extremely exposed position. Any abuse of my responsibility would not have been tolerated either by politicians or by the BBC.

But how have you managed to appear as a highly controversial and combative personality, without breaking the rules by which you claim your work is governed?
One is a matter of personal style, the other concerns editorial content and professional discipline. If that is not a satisfactory explanation, I really don't know how to explain it. The question is rather like asking a tightrope walker how he manages to keep his balance when so high up on such a thin wire. I don't see what answer he could give except

the blindingly obvious and singularly uninformative: 'Practice, Experience, Nerve, Instinct'.

You've been walking your tightrope for twenty years. Isn't that a long time to have kept your balance? Aren't you afraid of falling off?
If I do, there's no safety net, so I must try to stay up on the high-wire. 'Twenty years on a tightrope'. Now that you put it that way, I'm beginning to have nerves in retrospect. I hadn't thought of it as being quite so precarious. Remind me not to look down.

5. Redressing the Balance

From one of your first answers you seem to have become somewhat disenchanted with the way television is being used as a journalistic medium. Why?

My main reason is that television's coverage of events and treatment of issues can be dangerous and defective in certain fundamental respects. With its appetite for sensation and violence, its dependence on pictures, its pressures of time, television has a natural tendency to distort and to trivialize. Powerful though it is, that tendency must be resisted. Television journalism is now the main medium of mass communication in our democracy. Those in charge of it, those who work in it, can take pride in their achievements over the last twenty years. They have a great responsibility now to exercise self-restraint and self-discipline.

Incidentally, in referring to TV's 'appetite for violence', I am not here discussing the *fictional* violence of plays or films, though that is part of the picture. Fictional violence, realistically portrayed, is another influence which must be presumed to be potentially dangerous in various ways, but that is a different area in which I have no professional responsibility. It is a problem which has been widely discussed by others who are better qualified.

THE ADVANCE OF TV JOURNALISM

From your reference to 'achievements' you are not wholly disenchanted, despite the anxiety you have expressed?

By no means. Television journalism has made enormous progress in the last twenty years. The techniques and the technology have been improved and revolutionized. The vividness, the immediacy, the excitement of 'seeing it happen', has not diminished with familiarity. Colour, of an extremely high technical quality, has intensified the medium's hold on the viewer, and has enhanced its power of visual reporting. There is a much greater variety of journalistic output than there was twenty years ago. News programmes are longer and have become formidable competition to Fleet Street. ITN, under the editorship of Sir Geoffrey Cox, led the way in 1967 with its half-hour *News at Ten*. Newspapers have had to rethink their function and adapt their approach.

Events have been a testing challenge. More than anyone ever expected twenty years ago, the age of television journalism has been an age of war and violence. Great credit must go to television journalists—reporters, producers, cameramen, editors—for their coverage, often brilliant and courageous, of wars in Vietnam and in the Middle East, of Northern Ireland and of Cyprus.

Television's coverage of politics has made television part of politics, though the case for televising Parliament[1] has not yet been accepted. If the television cameras are admitted to the Commons, following the historic radio experiment in June 1975, television's contribution to the democratic process will be infinitely improved.

TELEVISION'S TABLOID TEMPTATIONS

Having said all that, my anxiety remains. The *momentum* of television's development has not always been matched by the *quality* of that development.

Five years ago my *Encounter* article 'The Troubled Reflections of a Television Journalist'[2] pointed to some of the inherent dangers and limitations in television as a medium of journalism. My concern was echoed by many thinking people, not only in this country but in America and other parts of the world. I was not the only person to be feeling that the tabloid medium of television appeals more to the emotions rather than to reason, and that its power to distort, to inflame and to trivialize, has dangerous implications for democracy.

What do you want to be done about it?
The first thing is for everybody concerned to recognize the dangers and to realize that what is called 'good' television may often amount to an

[1]See Part III, p. 117, for the arguments set out in my 1963 pamphlet 'The Case for Televising Parliament'.
[2]See Part II, p. 93, for reprint of *Encounter* article, May 1970.

irresponsible misuse of the power which television has. It is only fair to say that some awareness and concern exists and has increased in the last few years. But unless the dangers are fully understood and the tendencies clearly recognized they will not be effectively counteracted.

But if these dangers and tendencies are inherent in the nature and mechanics of the medium, how can they be counteracted now that television journalism has established its style and techniques so strongly?

Television, like the automobile or the computer, or nuclear explosive, can be used wisely or wickedly, responsibly or irresponsibly, destructively or constructively. In order that television may be used more wisely and more responsibly as a medium of information and opinion there are two lines of action to pursue. First: to minimize the harmful or unsatisfactory ways in which the various techniques and habits of television can affect the treatment of a subject. Secondly: accepting that those techniques and habits cannot be entirely swept away because they arise from the nature of the medium, we should seek to redress the balance in television's journalistic output by including more programme material which is deliberately designed to counteract the undesirable effects.

SOME BAD HABITS

How do you apply those two ideas, which may sound all very well as general principles, in the practical making of particular programmes?

Let me give some examples. Television journalism has a number of habits which are bad, and must be controlled. Like smoking, these habits are not easy to cut down, let alone give up. The worst habit of all is not allowing enough *time* for adequately serious treatment of a subject. I am only too aware that many interviews and other items may seem far too long, particularly those in which I happen to be appearing. That is a criticism of how the time is used and how the material is handled. Length is not a guarantee of quality. Time is not always a cure for triviality, but far too many items and programmes are far too short. They end when they have only just begun. They are an insult to the viewers, and to the participants. They are a contempt of the subject under consideration.

Another of the worst habits is *overcrowding* an item with too many people or too many points for discussion. Nobody has enough time to make their points. None of the issues are adequately discussed. The chairman has an impossible task. This overcrowding often arises from quite creditable intentions and because of certain pressures which are understandably hard to resist, even though the 'overcrowding' habit is known to be a bad one.

Can you deny that 'overcrowding' also arises from discreditable intentions as when a producer in collusion with the reporter sets out to mount a programme with lots of sound and fury?

No. I can't deny that. But I am trying to be fair. The point is that when programmes are being planned the genuine intention usually is to keep the number of participants and points to a manageable number. But somehow the numbers go up and up, and additional points for discussion creep in. The pressures which create this inflation are strong. The need for 'balance' and for adequate representation of this or that body of opinion is one of those pressures. Another well-intentioned reason for overcrowding is, ironically enough, the desire to avoid trivialization, by trying to cover the subject as thoroughly as possible. The result may often be a shambles, or at best a disconnected series of snippety remarks. All the producer has achieved is the trivialization he wanted to avoid.

Is not overcrowding sometimes due to the inevitable pressure which must affect any kind of journalism—the need to cut down one item so as to include another one at the last minute?

That is true. But a newspaper story can be cut or compressed without fatal sacrifice of intelligibility or fairness. A 'live' television item is a very different kettle of fish. The item may have been sensibly planned in good faith for, say, twenty minutes in which five participants discussing three main points would be reasonably manageable. But cut down to fifteen minutes, shortly before you go up to the studio, the item can become a shameful farce. One of the key points is never covered. The other two are skimped. The participants feel they have been misled. The viewers have been served a dud. The luckless chairman blows his top to the producer. He goes home with a sense of depression and guilt at having been mixed up in the whole wretched business.

One of the troubles is that item lengths are often overestimated in the first place, either because of optimism or lack of frankness. That first generous length is apt to be 'adjusted' as the clock gets nearer to transmission time. Those seventeen promised minutes suddenly turn out to include a three-and-a-half minute introduction.

Would you deny, however, that you have sometimes overcome this prob-lem by exceeding the allotted time and ignoring the clearest possible time-signals?
Disobey Mother! What a monstrous suggestion.

What has your mother to do with it?
Not *my* mother. I am referring to a formidable lady called Miss Joan Marsden.

Miss Marsden is a mother?
Oh dear. No. She is the lady who has been the floor-manager in almost all my programmes, and is affectionately known as 'Mother' to ever-body involved from studio technicians to visiting statesmen. She com-mands a studio full of difficult men in a way which would be not unworthy of the Virgin Queen and her noblemen, or Margaret Thatcher and her Shadow Cabinet.

Nevertheless you have on occasion ignored her clear and emphatic signals?
I don't like the word 'ignore'. Let us say that I have sometimes inter-preted her signals in a way which takes into account my obligation to conclude the item fairly, or to remember the producer's instruction that such and such a point *must* be covered.

But on these occasions do you experience some difficulty in seeing the time-signals?
In the heat of a difficult programme this has been known to happen. As with Nelson at the Battle of Copenhagen.

In fairness will you also admit that though some items may prove un-manageably short, your time has sometimes been generously extended?
Yes, and on such occasions I do not shrink from the added duty demanded of me.

And do you ever, even in the heat of a difficult programme, experience any
difficulty in seeing the signals to extend *the time?*
Never. The signals are even clearer to me than usual on those occasions.
I recall one programme with particular relish, a late-night discussion
about the seamen's strike in 1966: the strike in which Mr Wilson made
his famous reference to a 'tightly-knit group of politically motivated
men'. We had them on the programme and I was allowed to overrun
for, I think, twenty-seven minutes. That was a rare pleasure. Eventually
the only way to end it was to pull my camera away to the other side of
the studio for the anchorman's 'Goodnight'.

THE CRAVING FOR 'PACE'

Could we get back to the bad habits?
The deplorable habits of 'overcrowding' and of not allowing sufficient
time are closely connected with another habit which television journalists suffer from, and must control: the craving for what is called *'pace'* or
'moving it along'.

The craving for 'pace' comes from a belief that nothing on a television screen can hold the viewers' attention for more than a very few
minutes, unless it is some compulsively watchable happening. Even if
this is true, and I remain unconvinced that it is universally true, whoever
is running the programme must not allow it to undermine his duty to
the subject. He should forget unproven assumptions about viewer
psychology, summon up his courage, and strike a responsible balance
between the risk of boring the viewer and the risk of trivializing the
subject. It may well be that more viewers are infuriated by an item
being cut off in the middle, than by its continuing to a more reasonable
length. Too often, however, the craving for 'pace' is too strong to
resist. This means that even a long programme of an hour or more,
which is intended to cover a subject thoroughly, may defeat its own
object by being broken up in to little bits and pieces, each of which is
superficial and overcrowded with participants.

These and other bad habits of television journalism can and must be
controlled. They do not only occur in current affairs programmes.
The news on television, even though it is now longer, frequently suffers
from too many brief and superficial items, and from over-emphasizing
the importance of film which happens to be visually exciting. The

greater length of the *Nine o'clock News* on BBC 1 and of *News at Ten* has sometimes resulted in greater depth, but too often there is merely a larger number of short items. One of the bad effects is that apart from the main stories, which are done in some detail, the items dealt with in brief are often so baldly summarized that the meaning may not be apparent until one reads a newspaper next morning.

PRIORITIES IN TV NEWS

There must be a stronger resistance to the distortion of television news values by the pictorial demands of the medium. The selection and order of news items seems too often to be dictated not by their importance, but by the availability of visually exciting film. The news values of television, transmitted into every home every night, must be sober, balanced and responsible. If they continually overemphasize the violent, the sensational and the trivial, whether for pictorial reasons or because of an urge to be parochial or 'popular', television will be a corrupting and degrading influence on all our thoughts and attitudes. The audiences for television news are enormous. They include vast numbers of children and young people. No one has any right to assume that the values of television news today will not exert a powerful influence on the values of society tomorrow.

I do not for one moment suggest that television news should deliberately omit the violence and sensation. That would be to suppress the truth and to distort the news. Television journalists cannot stop the world even if they want to get off. What I am suggesting is that violence and sensation are not always the most significant aspects of the news. They do not necessarily have to be given priority by television. Furthermore, there is a choice of ways in which a violent or sensational happening can be reported on the screen, as television journalists are well aware. It can be presented with varying degrees of pictorial emphasis, all consistent with true and factual reporting. One of my former Editors, the wise Sir Geoffrey Cox, used to turn the famous maxim of C. P. Scott into one for television: 'Facts are sacred but presentation is free.' That freedom of presentation, in the visual medium of television, must be used with restraint and responsibility, especially in news programmes.

Are you advocating even longer news programmes than at present?
Yes. The major news programme should be longer than its present twenty-five minutes or so, but it should also be transformed into a new and much more comprehensive 'newspaper of the screen'. This should be an hour in length, with deeper and wider coverage of news and current affairs, the precise distinction between which has never been clear to me. The 'Hour of News' is a separate proposal which I would like to explain and defend later.[1]

TOOLS, NOT TOYS

Let me make one or two further points about the techniques of television journalism. These are not necessarily harmful in themselves. What concerns me is that they are liable to be used in a way which lowers the level of argument, distorts the issues, emphasizes the violent, and focuses on the emotive.

Television journalists have at their disposal a fascinating variety of techniques and visual aids by which to present and illustrate their material. Apart from straightforward studio pictures and film, there are animated graphics, cartoons, studio set designs, maps, models, lighting arrangements, and so on. These should be used for two purposes only: to make the transmitted material more clear, and to make it more interesting. They are tools, not toys. Visual aids should not be used as visual gimmicks. They are facilities to aid presentation, not to dominate content. The mechanics of the medium should not be allowed to distort the message.

There are various ways of using the studio. An audience can be brought in, to put questions or to add reality to the argument. In either case the result may be an atmosphere of entertainment or emotional outburst. I remember a programme on the death penalty. Amid the argument the cameras suddenly closed in on a relative, highly distraught, of a recently murdered man. I had intense sympathy for that relative, not merely because of the tragedy suffered, but because personal distress appeared to be exploited to make 'good television', even though the honest intention may simply have been to illustrate the argument in real and human terms. I may have been wrong to shudder, but that was the effect on me and on many others.

[1] See pp. 62–74.

Isn't there a strong case for saying that in a subject like the death penalty, ordinary human reactions, however distressing, are essential in television discussion, to lift it out of the rut of abstract argument?

That is a fair point. It is very hard to define when the televising of personal anguish is legitimate (or indeed essential) in order to show an essential fact of an argument or situation, and when it amounts to the exploitation of personal anguish for the purpose of achieving 'good television' or 'compulsive viewing'. Judgment on this will depend on the atmosphere and tone of the particular programme. The wrong kind of atmosphere is more likely to be built up if there is a large studio audience.

THE STUDIO AUDIENCE

Studio audiences may often defeat their object, which is to achieve a representative expression of views from a variety of people. What can easily happen is that the programme degenerates into a bear-garden atmosphere in which few people have a chance to say anything effectively and the argument is hopelessly confused. This is not the fault of the audience, many of whom will go home with a bitter sense of frustration. It is partly the fault of those who arrange or conduct the programme, and partly due to the simple fact of having an audience in a television studio. For most of the audience it is a first-time visit. There is an exciting sense of occasion. For some it is an outing—a trip to London for instance. The inside workings of the telly are on view. A well-known 'TV personality' is there in the flesh. Other famous people may be present. Autographs are requested and given. All perfectly natural, but hardly the atmosphere conducive to a serious and considered discussion.

Another technique is to have an audience vote—a kind of mini-referendum or instant opinion-poll. This can have precious little validity and merely serves as a way of providing a 'result' to hold audience interest. The vote, moreover, may be taken on some preconceived question which has been shown by what clear discussion there may have been to be either loaded, or a crude over-simplification.

I am not arguing that there should never be a studio audience, nor that such programmes should never be angry or heated. As a BBC document points out[1]:

'. . . the producer cannot lose sight of the fact that to suppress passions which exist as factors in the controversy may do a disservice to his audience equal to the suppression of reasoned argument.'

That is right. But so far as studio audiences are concerned they are more likely, through no fault of their own, to result in passion, noise and incoherence at the expense of reasoned argument.

GIMMICKS AND GADGETRY

Audiences, as I have said, are only one of the many techniques of current affairs programmes in television. These techniques are all capable of being used to achieve a jazzed-up or sexed-up presentation. The justification is that it is done to 'grab them', an ugly piece of professional jargon which means to win the viewers' interest. This is legitimate so long as it does not involve distortion and over-simplification, which so often occurs particularly in the introductions to items.

Similarly film reports or shorter film-clips by way of illustration can be used responsibly or tendentiously, according to how the film is selected and edited. Graphics and animated illustrations of various kinds can be of great value. They can also serve to distract, to confuse, and to over-simplify. Even if they are brilliantly done, they may be so vivid and ingenious that they may obscure the points they are supposed to make clearer.

Great trouble is taken over designing studio sets. Here again a balance must be struck between something which gives style and identity to the programme without obtruding, and something which is so elaborate and stagey that it distracts attention from the content of the programme. That kind of set may even lead the director to plan his studio camera shots in a way which is aimed more at showing off the set and the physical interrelation of the participants, than at concentrating on what the programme is really about. The skill of the director, who controls the cameras and calls the shots, can make or

[1] *Taste and Standards in BBC Programmes*—a study by the BBC for its General Advisory Council; published 1973.

mar a programme. I do not underestimate the skill required. But a television studio with all its apparatus and paraphernalia should, in current affairs programmes, be used with restraint and simplicity. That requires a subtler skill and judgment than in using it for theatrical gadgetry.

Television journalists may, with every justification, use their skills to present a serious subject entertainingly, but not as entertainment. Producers and reporters should not become so dazzled by their array of television techniques that they lose sight of television's duty to be fair and factual. There is a sarcastic piece of professional jargon which refers to the more straightforward kind of presentation. It is called 'letting the facts get in the way of the story'.

People who come into television journalism from outside often see the dangers more clearly than those whose entire professional experience has been involved in television programme-making. After my 'Troubled Reflections' had appeared in *Encounter*,[1] I received an even more troubled letter from someone who had worked for a time in the production team of a well-known topical programme. I need not mention its name, or the network, because the writer's anxiety is relevant to what goes on in a good many television production offices. If I may quote from that letter:

'If current affairs producers (and even more so news producers) don't take care they may lose control of the medium, which has a strong inherent momentum in the direction you indicate. Current affairs coverage could become so showbiz that it's a public *dis*service. Television should serve its material and not the other way round. It is the evening medium and for many people now, the only source of serious "current affairs" journalism. Producers must recognize that most important developments are not primarily visual, and should be treated at least as much in their own terms as in television's, if viewers are not to be misinformed and miseducated. It seems to me that it is very hard to inform, educate *and* entertain simultaneously. All too often, the result misinforms, miseducates and fails to entertain.'

From that I would pick out two key points: 'Television should serve its material and not the other way round' and 'Producers must

[1]See Part II, pp. 93–114.

recognize that most important developments are not primarily visual.'
If these two principles are put into practice, and are not merely spoken
of approvingly, we shall have done much to minimize the tendencies
and temptations which exist in television journalism.

COUNTERACTION

*Even if these principles are effectively applied, the balance of television
journalism will, as you have admitted, still be naturally tilted towards an
emotively visual emphasis. How should we achieve the second of your
objects which was to redress that balance?*

The way to redress the balance is to ensure that television's journalistic
output includes more programme material which is primarily concerned with rational discussion and inquiry. This should deal particularly with those issues, ideas, or events which otherwise might not
receive adequate emphasis or explanation. The broad aim of redressing
the balance in this way is to counteract what is described in my *Encounter*
article as the 'dangerous and increasing concentration by television
journalism, on action (usually violent and bloody) rather than on
thought, on happenings rather than issues, on shock rather than on
explanation, on personalities rather than ideas'.[1]

There is already some awareness of what is needed. On all three
television channels there are programmes whose aim is reasoned
argument and serious analysis. Too many of these programmes, however, have a limited value in redressing the balance because they are
transmitted at a very late hour, or on a minority channel, or are not
networked. The balance will not be effectively redressed unless it is
further redressed for the *main* audience.

Here let me emphasize that I am not referring to the general balance
of *all* television programmes—plays, news, movies, documentaries,
sport, arts, light entertainment, current affairs. I am discussing the
balance only within television's treatment of news and current affairs,
and the need for more material which put the emphasis on reasoned
explanation and serious inquiry.

[1]See Part II, p. 96.

'No thanks, cabbie, it just so happens that I don't want to hear your views on the Common Market.'

But whatever you may advocate, would the audience like it? If it was aimed at the mass-audience would there not be a mass switch-off?

I do not expect the vast numbers which watch *Miss World* or *Match of the Day*. But some very substantial audiences (larger than the circulation of a popular newspaper) have been won for serious programmes mounted at good times on the main channel. For example in 1971 there was a *three-hour* debate on BBC 1 about the Common Market. This was The Great Debate, described by me (in a moment of exasperation of which I am frequently reminded) as the 'great cock-up' when the voting computer went wrong at the end. Of the 5½ million who saw the start at 9.20 p.m., 3½ million were still watching at half-past midnight. Those are huge figures, and nobody would call the Common Market a sexy subject.

But is it fair to pick out what was a single special programme, boosted by unusual publicity?

I think so, because it shows what can be done in a mass-audience programme. As for a series of programmes, may I mention one which set out to redress the balance and won high audience appreciation. I refer to the three-part *Sunday Debates* which began in 1973 on BBC 1.

THE SUNDAY DEBATES

These were welcomed by many in television and outside as a refreshing contrast to the noise and incoherence which had become so predictable on the box. Some of the younger people in television were among the most enthusiastic. The formula which I had suggested for *Sunday Debate* (with each subject spread over three Sundays) was designed to achieve fairness, clarity and stimulating argument. There were three principles. First: that the participants should each have a fair opportunity to state their case clearly and without interruption. Second, that the arguments should be met not only by counter-argument but by critical examination. Third: that the formal structure of the programme would, as in court proceedings or well-constructed drama, produce some climatic moments of intellectual conflict and personal performance which would grip the viewers' interest without obscuring or trivializing the issues.

The young producer, Mr David Kennard, immediately grasped the possibilities with imagination, and realized what could be achieved. We continued to modify and improve the format throughout the series. There was, however, one problem which we never quite overcame. Although the total time for each subject was over an hour and a half, each of the three programmes was only thirty to thirty-five minutes. This was liable to be overcrowded by our carefully-contrived structure of statements and cross-examination.

The series covered a number of social and moral issues, from immigration to trade union power. By being clear and fair and orderly, it helped a little to 'redress the balance'. At the same time it was not lacking in visual interest or excitement. That was its significance: to show that rational television can also be 'good' television. Some people were quite surprised.

How does your case for more of these long, serious, in-depth programmes square with your argument that Panorama *should be a mixture of shorter items, rather than a single-subject programme?*
I did not argue that *Panorama* should *never* be a single-subject programme. I've done many, and have admired those of others. My argument was that it should not *always* be a single-subject programme, either on film or in the studio. I advocated the reasonable mixture, with flexibility and topicality, which had become the familiar and well-liked *Panorama* style. That does not conflict with my arguments for 'redressing the balance' in television journalism. I have referred to programmes of an hour's length or more only because they happened to be major examples. A twenty-minute item (in *Panorama* or any other programme) may certainly help to 'redress the balance' in reason's favour. Length can help a great deal, but I repeat: length is not a guarantee of quality or clarity. Time does not necessarily prevent the trivial. What really matters is the integrity.

INTEGRITY IN FILM MAKING

Are you interested in any other ways, apart from studio programmes, of redressing the balance in television journalism?
So far I've referred only to studio programmes, such as debates and interviews. If well-conceived and well-conducted, those are the programmes which most obviously embody the idea of rational discussion

and serious inquiry, as opposed to the more emotive and visually-sensational kind of programme. Film programmes also have an indispensable part to play. There are many aspects of current events which can only be adequately dealt with by filmed reports, inquiries and documentaries. But just as studio programmes can degenerate into the trivial and the sensational, so can film. If film programmes are to help redress the balance they must be made and edited with scrupulous integrity, in both technique and content. They must be made and edited in a way which does justice to those who may appear in the film—the the coal-miner, the businessman, the nurse, the coloured immigrant, and, yes, even the despised politician. Films must also do justice to the public who watch, and who are entitled to trust in the film-maker's integrity.

The tricks which may be legitimate in the cinema have no place in television journalism. There should be no faking, no ingenious creation of illusions, no staging of situations, no exploitation of emotion or violence for box-office reasons. In making films, television journalists have a magnificent opportunity to use the power of this visual medium honestly and fairly. They also have a terrible temptation to use it corruptly and tendentiously. That temptation must be resisted. Those responsible must see that they resist it.

The television organizations, notably the BBC, have their codes of rules and principles for the making of film reports and documentaries. In the rush and tension of programme-making, in the individual's zeal for a cause, in the temptation to get a cheap laugh at someone's expense, under the pressure created by television's appetite for visual sensation, these rules come under strain. They must be even more vigilantly enforced.

PLAYING IT HOT, AND PLAYING IT COOL

Will not the general theme of your argument—redressing the balance in favour of reason—seem curiously unrealistic to many of your readers? How can television journalists ignore the existence of passion and prejudice, anger and hatred, brutality and violence?

Manifestly, they cannot do so. I have not suggested that they should. Their first duty is to truth. But they have another duty: to make and present responsibly a selection from what is true. Television's coverage of events and issues should be presented in a way which does not distort, which does not sensationalize, and which does not inflame. Television journalism can do all these things. Whatever television touches, it can magnify, inflate, project, and spread. Such power should be put on the side of reason, without which our civilization will sink into barbarism.

Are you not putting it rather too portentously?
If you say so, although one doesn't have to look far to see the barbarism even now. But let me be less portentous: television journalists can play it hot, and they can play it cool. They should make more effort to play it cool.

6. The Reasonable Society

You talk of reason. But can there not be reasoned justification of violence and terrorism, of inhumanity and hatred?

There is indeed no shortage of such twisted logic. The sectarian murderer in Belfast will claim to have reasoned justification for his crimes. To the perverted mind of Hitler there may have seemed to be reasoned justification for Auschwitz. So what?

Then what kind of reason do you want television to uphold? That which commends itself to your values, your concept of society?

Certainly. I have only one life to live and only one country I wish to live it in. In this country, we do not live in a valueless moral vacuum, like astronauts floating weightless in a lunar spacecraft. We are entrusted with a set of values through which our reasoning is tempered with humanity, moderated by fairness, based on truth, imbued with the Christian ethic, applied with commonsense, and upheld by law. If there is a gulf of hypocrisy between the professing and the practice of those values, that does not mean that we should abandon them.

What I am arguing will be regarded with contempt and derision by certain people, including some in the media and in the universities. There are those who devote their minds and their activities to propagating a very different set of ideas: that the Rule of Law is bourgeois establishment oppression, that parliamentary government is ritualized hypocrisy, that peaceful co-operation with the democratic system is surrender to the prevailing power-structure, that criminal violence of the most bestial kind can be morally justifiable. If you start being intellectually seduced by that kind of argument, then you are on the road to nothing but the jungle. In the absence of a world rule of law, the nation states of the world are still marching on that road. But within nation states, or at least within *our* nation state which is what matters to me, we have chosen the path of reason, to establish that civilized order which is liberty under law, and government by consent.

Of late, that civilized order has been increasingly threatened by unreason and lawlessness, violence and terrorism. Television may well have been, if not the cause, a contributing influence. By reflecting, television may have inflamed. By depicting, television may have magnified. By projecting, television may have incited. By accentuating, television may have encouraged.

TELEVISION AND THE REASONABLE SOCIETY

You say may have encouraged, may have incited. Does that not show you are condemning without proof, and (if I may throw the word back at you) without reason?

I have no conclusive proof. Nor can sociologists offer any clear evidence one way or the other. That does not mean we should shut our eyes and think nothing. I am entitled to the reasonable doubts of a reasonable man. Unless there is convincing proof to the contrary, it is entirely reasonable that we should work on the presumption that television may be an influence in the direction of unreason and violence. We owe it to ourselves and to future generations to work on that presumption. We must see that television's influence is turned in the direction of reason and non-violence. Many disturbing trends and events should have now made us more resolute to uphold the Reasonable Society, with its balance between freedom and order, which we have taken for granted for so long. Our resolution should have some expression in our television.

Television does not belong to itself, it is ours. Television in this country, both public service and commercial, exists and operates only by the community's authority given by the democratic will of Parliament. To speed the disintegration of that community, to hasten the slide into unreason and violence, is no part of television's duty. It should give no avoidable encouragement to what Russell called 'the anti-rational philosophy of naked will'.

Television should be biased in favour of reason.

Television should sustain the Reasonable Society, together with its parliamentary institutions.

Would the BBC agree with that opinion, and with your view of television's responsibility to the parliamentary system which gives it existence?

I would not presume to speak for the Corporation, which speaks with its own wisdom on these matters. But I would respectfully endorse the clear and unequivocal statement of Sir Michael Swann, Chairman of the Board of Governors: 'Because parliamentary democracy is the necessary precondition of the BBC's independence, we have a particular incentive to preserve it, over and above our incentive as citizens.'[1]

DANGERS TO DEMOCRACY

Is not all your talk about the Reasonable Society and its parliamentary institutions liable to sound complacent? Is not our society extremely unreasonable, with much deprivation, inequality and social injustice? Is not democracy itself in danger from the forces of violence and inflation?

The whole theme of my argument is the very opposite of complacent. I have said we must be more resolute to uphold what is in danger. I am deeply concerned that television's power should sustain the Reasonable Society.

In using that phrase I am drawing attention to something which is in peril—a kind of society which, whatever its present troubles, is by nature and tradition reasonable in the way it lives and governs itself. That way is by peaceful reform rather than violent revolution. For all that we have to be ashamed of or anxious about now, we have only to look at what enormous social and economic progress we have made in these islands during the last hundred years, without bloodshed, under the much-abused parliamentary system which is the cornerstone of the Reasonable Society.

Present dangers are very great. We are smitten with two forms of madness and unreason: violence or the use of force in one degree or another, and inflation which threatens to destroy not only the value of our money, but the fabric of our society. If the Reasonable Society and its institutions are to survive, we must be vigilant to uphold it. I have urged that television should play its part more positively, by restraint, by self-discipline, by responsible use of its mass influence, and by redressing its balance in favour of reason and understanding.

What is the difference between what you call the Reasonable Society and

[1]Speech to the Royal Television Society, October 22nd 1974. Reprinted as a BBC pamphlet: 'The Autonomy of the Broadcaster'.

what is known as the liberal-democratic society? Why choose a new name?
There have been many concepts identified or propagated by the multiplicity of labels coupled historically with the word 'society': Open, Great, Christian, Free, Socialist, Capitalist, Democratic, Liberal, Affluent, Permissive, Corporate, and so on. The Reasonable Society is more than a system of government or economics or religion. It is an idea which embraces the temper and disposition of a society, its character and values.

THE IDEA OF THE REASONABLE SOCIETY

The United States of America has a liberal-democratic constitution, but it is not an example of what I mean by the Reasonable Society. A liberal-democratic system may involve the uglier forms of capitalism, with crude materialism and violent social tensions.

So may the social democratic idea (according to what concept of social democracy prevails) involve an unreasonable degree of statism and bureaucratic suffocation of the individual. How far any version of social democracy is consistent with the Reasonable Society must depend on how far the power of the state is extended, how far egalitarianism is imposed; and also on what solution is found to the crucial conflict (which Professor Vaizey sees in his analysis[1] of Social Democracy as one of its greatest difficulties) arising from financial dependence on and historical links with trade unions.

The Reasonable Society transcends and cuts across established politico-economic systems and the crude division between the ideologies of left and right. It involves a way of thinking which is relevant to, and should pervade, many other aspects of life and thought. For example, the effect of economic growth on the quality of life; the search for a devolution policy which would prevent rather than precipitate the break-up of the United Kingdom; the dangers to press freedom from certain kinds of trade union action; the future of the middle class; the influence on the cultural atmosphere of commercialized brutality, ugliness, and sheer animalism; the balance in sexual matters between private freedom and social well-being; problems in education

[1] *Social Democracy*, by John Vaizey. Praeger Publishers Inc, 1972.

and in race relations. The list could flow on into many other areas of potentially bitter conflict, where what is needed is not prejudice, not obdurate partisanship, not fanatical adherence to a particular view of progress or freedom, but reasonableness and moderation.

In the Reasonable Society there can be no place for absolutes, no place for theories which must be rigidly adhered to, no place for dogmas which must be defended to the death. The tragedy of Ulster has grown out of absolutes and dogmas, the seed-beds of unreason and violence. There should be no principle which is too important to be reconsidered for the sake of others, no interest which cannot make some sacrifice for the common good, no conflict which cannot be solved without the use of force or law-breaking; and—if I may venture into a sacred area—no *sport* which need be taken quite as seriously as *war*, either by players or spectators.

Otherwise we will be turning our backs on the Reasonable Society and we will be dragged down into something much uglier.

CHARACTER AND CLIMATE

The idea of the Reasonable Society is deeply rooted in our temper and tradition. That temper and tradition has much in common with our climate. It does not go to the uttermost extremes. The barometer may go up and down, but it never registers a cataclysm. Perhaps our equable character has some direct connection with our equable climate; and also perhaps with the quality of light and colour which goes with that climate. To a visitor from a country where the climate is fierce, where the sun and sky are harsh and brilliant, the English light is gentle and the colours have a certain softness—the qualities of light and colour captured with such magical effect by the genius of our greatest painter, Turner, in his landscapes.

Before you wax too romantic about the British colour scheme and climate, would not your visitor's prevailing impression be that it is grey, dull, wet and chilly?
Perhaps, but don't forget all those 'bright intervals', which do not always prove to be figments of the weatherman's imagination. Think of a London park on a fine spring morning. Anway, though the connection may be imaginary, our character, like our climate, is temperate.

It is not given to violent storms of tropical force or to revolutionary cyclones. We can become fairly heated, but not to such a scorching temperature as to be easily combustible. We are a mild people, mild of manner, mild of disposition and mild of method, except when we are roused, which is rare.

The Reasonable Society, and the institutions which have grown with it, has flowered in the temperate climate of our mental habits. Equanimity is preferred to hysteria. Experience is a wiser guide than doctrine. Absolutes are alien to us. We know that absolute equality would extinguish liberty; that absolute liberty would demolish order. We shrink from extreme measures. We harden ourselves to take them if we must, though sometimes we are almost too late. Humour, both coarse and subtle, is part of our very being. Humour is our sense of proportion. Our sense of proportion is the essence of our reasonableness.

Why do you think it relevant to tell us all this, which may appear to some of your readers as little more than a string of platitudes?
Anyone who is inclined to dismiss what I have said as platitudinous should first remember that there are elements among us which would regard it as highly provocative. What we could have regarded as platitude until fairly recently is by no means so today. The characteristics of our way of doing things can no longer be taken for granted. Certain forces in our society are purposively in conflict with them. My feeling is, and this is the relevance, that television tends to strengthen those forces, not with any conscious purpose behind it, but because of its inherent tendencies as a medium. There can be seen in television an intense and frenetic quality, an emotiveness and heat, which threatens to affect the cool and temperate climate of our ideas and institutions.

THE INSTITUTIONS OF THE REASONABLE SOCIETY

That is why I think it is worthwhile reminding ourselves of what those ideas and institutions mean. Whether our institutions have shaped us, or we our institutions, their essential characteristic is reasonableness, rather than logical theory or perfection. Trial by jury, for example, where liberty depends on the verdict of ordinary citizens. The common law, built up case by case for a thousand years, takes as its practical guide the Reasonable Man, the 'man on the Clapham omnibus'.

Constitutional monarchy, evolved in the struggles of the past, stands as a pre-eminently reasonable compromise: pageantry without power, continuity consistent with change. And returning to our muttons, the British system of broadcasting has been a classic example of the reasonable approach. On one side the BBC, a public service yet without state control. On the other side a commercial service yet publicly regulated. An arrangement under which each side benefits in different ways from the competing presence of the other.

Parliament is the supreme example. In reasonable proportions, it is both workshop and theatre. Both are necessary. Most of the time it is a workshop, for legislation and inquiry. For a little of the time, it is a theatre of debate, about issues, policies and personalities. As a theatre of debate, Parliament may seem to present an excess of farce and to stage too many set-piece battles. But it would not be reasonable if silliness, noise, abuse, and anger were totally non-existent in an assembly of several hundred free men and women. On the day there is vulgar uproar in the Kremlin we shall know that freedom is on its way in Russia.

There may seem to be unreasonable behaviour over points of procedure. But trivial though they may be in themselves, points of procedure often involve points of principle. They are parliamentary weapons of protest. Better a point of procedure than a petrol-bomb.

Though the rowdier parliamentary 'scenes' make the headlines, the truth is that a central quality of Parliament is the reasonableness and mutual courtesy with which most of its business is conducted. The bitterness of political conflict among fellow parliamentarians is softened by private civilities and personal confidences. These, of course, are said to symbolize the 'hypocrisy of the Party charade'. They do not. They are reasonable and civilized behaviour.

Of course Parliament needs reform. It has always needed reform, and always will. It has been reforming itself for more than seven hundred years. The process will continue, in a reasonable way and at a reasonable speed.

THE GABBLE-SHOP AND THE GUN-BARREL

Men of intellectual brilliance have often scoffed at Parliament. My good and gifted friend Mr Bernard Levin, reaching for his adjectival automatic, has described the House of Commons as a 'mob of roaring, boring, jabbering, gibbering, bawling, squalling, perfectly appalling hooligans'. A somewhat exaggerated description, even of Parliament at its most unruly, but let that pass. Mr Levin is not the first genius to misunderstand Parliament. Long before Bernard Levin, there was Bernard Shaw, with 'That foolish gabble-shop'.

Mao Tse-Tung has told us that 'Political power grows out of the barrel of a gun'. In the Reasonable Society, there are some of us who prefer power from a gabble-shop than from a gun-barrel. Better the theatre of debate, than the theatre of violence.

The Reasonable Society is not, as may be thought, merely a convenient idea to play about with in argument. It is fundamentally indispensable to the practical working of the British system of democracy. This is because we have no written constitution, no fundamental law to be applied, no judicial review by a supreme court, no basic rights engraved in marble. It is arguable that we should move towards such a constitution, as advocated by Lord Justice Scarman and Lord Hailsham. But for the time being, and for the foreseeable future, our constitution is expressed in six unwritten words: 'The Queen in Parliament is supreme'. Such a constitution has only worked, and can only work, with the accompaniment of the conventions, traditions, customs, compromises, voluntary restraints and the national sense of fair play, all of which go to make up the Reasonable Society.

But as a member of the EEC, do we not live under a fundamental law which is superior to Parliament?
Only within the Treaty limits, and by the authority of Parliament itself. But even that does not mean that Parliament has abandoned its sovereignty irrevocably and for ever. After all, the referendum in June 1975 was about whether we should withdraw. There was no question but that we have the power to withdraw, and that Parliament has the power to enact our withdrawal.

But we must return to the subject of television which, you may remember, we were discussing.

7. Transforming TV News

In what you have called 'redressing the balance' in television's coverage of news and current affairs, you advocated the 'transformation' of the news programmes. Why, and in what way?

This is fundamental. Television news is now the basic source of information on public events for many millions of people. The news programmes on both channels have vastly improved during the last twenty years. The main programmes (the *Nine o'clock News* on BBC1, and *News at Ten* from ITN) are among the most popular mass-audience viewing, despite the gloom and disaster which they so often present. They are crisply edited, well-presented and fast-moving. Particular credit is due to the *News at Ten* team for presenting their programmes with a sense of intelligent excitement and enthusiasm, especially on a night of 'big' news, but without loss of authority.

However, as the main source of news to so many millions, television news programmes could be greatly improved. At the moment they are a tabloid kaleidoscope of events—the televisual version of a newspaper's front page headlines, with only a fraction of the story content. Though the main facts are covered, their news value is liable to be affected by an over-emphasis on what is available by way of direct visual coverage of events. This tends to be edited so as to select the most visibly emotive or violent part for transmission.

Interviews, except on rare occasions, can be little more than perfunctory, without any real journalistic probing. Items which are difficult to cover in a visually exciting way—such as major economic development or an important debate in Parliament—have to be dealt with more briefly than their content deserves, and often too briefly to be adequately understood. It is quite common that a television news item has given the bare facts, but is so short on explanation as to make it little more than a signal to find out what it means in tomorrow morning's newspapers.

In general, therefore, television news is open to this criticism: that the very professionalism with which the material is presented televisually, narrows and distorts its news values. This affects the order, the length, the adequacy and the comprehensibility of the items. To re-quote a key point from the letter I referred to earlier[1]: 'Most important developments are not primarily visual.' This is not sufficiently recognized in the values and priorities which have become so characteristic of television news.

TV NEWS: THE DISTORTING MIRROR

But are not many important news developments 'primarily visual'? To give only three examples: the assassination of President Kennedy, the shooting on 'Bloody Sunday', and the entry of the Russian tanks into Prague? And for an example which is non-political, but of immediate importance to millions—a goal scored in the Cup Final?

The phrase was '*most* important developments are not primarily visual'. Not *all*. On such occasions and many others, when the really important news is primarily visual, television comes into its own. The newspapers cannot then compete, except by greater background detail, 'inside' stories, and interpretative comment. What I am pointing out is that the tendency of television news is to foster the impression that non-visual developments are as such less important. This means that in the news programmes, television's mirror of society and of the world is liable to reflect a distorted image.

Could it not be argued that television's priorities should be judged in a broader context, the availability of three different news media: the printed medium of the press, the oral medium of radio, and the visual medium of television? Does not each medium complement the other and possess its own special advantages over the other? Is not the vividness of 'seeing it happen' on television complemented by the printed news of the press which can be more detailed and analytical, and by radio news with its world-wide immediacy and uncluttered clarity?

That argument has considerable force, but for several reasons it does

[1]See p. 47.

not diminish the importance of 'redressing the balance' in television journalism and in television news in particular. Firstly: television is now the main mass medium of news. The shortcomings of television cannot therefore be overlooked, whatever the compensatory merits of the press and radio. Secondly: the vast majority of the television audience take popular papers which have tended to accept some of television's values, and whose news coverage is often crude and sensational. Thirdly: of the three media, television has by far the greatest power to emphasise and project those trends in our society which are dangerous and disturbing—disorder, violence, and disruption.

THE INSATIABLE APPETITE OF TELEVISION

These are staple ingredients of television's diet. Television's appetite for them is insatiable, and must be controlled. Nor must we forget that television's lust for visible action and 'happenings' is itself an invitation to create more visible action and happenings which can be projected on television. Television thrives on unreason, and unreason thrives on television.

Have you evidence to support that rather sweeping statement?
There are innumerable cases of situations being created and demonstrations being staged in a way which has been deliberately calculated to attract the television cameras and to achieve a place in the television news. If some individual or group wishes to protest about a grievance or a cause, the publicity they will get by achieving television coverage is infinitely bigger than by writing to the newspapers or addressing a public meeting. The way to attract television coverage is not by reasoned protest or persuasion, but by physical action of a spectacular kind such as a sit-in, a sit-down, an occupation or a provocatively staged march or demonstration.

But are not these activities a perfectly legitimate part of our democratic liberty?
That depends on the facts of each case and how peaceful the activity is. Sometimes they are within the law, sometimes not. Such activities can,

moreover, easily lead to other and more violent happenings which may be serious offences against the criminal law. The more violent and the more provocative they become, the more likely they are to get television news coverage.

Those being your misgivings about television news, how would you 'transform' it?

The first thing, as I have been arguing, is that the inherent temptations of television to distort its news values must be resisted. This should be done as far as is reasonably consistent with the visual nature of the medium. I accept that television news will always be, and should always be, different in character from the news as presented on the printed page or in a radio bulletin.

Now we come to the transformation which in my opinion is necessary if television news is to give better service to the public, and to make more responsible use of the medium. No matter how carefully and responsibly edited, the present length and style of television news programmes will be defective in a number of important respects. It will be lacking in background explanation. It will be lacking in the probing element of good interviewing, and the element of investigation which can be achieved in good film reporting. It will be lacking in the element of argument and discussion to illuminate an issue or to reflect an important conflict of principles or personalities. It will have insufficient time and space to ensure that the visually exciting or emotive material, which must be accepted in these times as an inescapable part of television news, is at least balanced by the accompanying inclusion of explanation, analysis and inquiry.

As one kind of example: if there is an angry industrial dispute the television news will show the stormy scenes which have occurred, coupled with a brief report by the industrial correspondent and a brief interview with a leading figure on one side or both. An extended television news would also seek to include a reasoned, clarifying analysis by way of discussion or interview with a well-illustrated explanation of the facts and figures which would be much clearer than what we usually get at present in the news programmes. Explanatory discussion and analysis is generally left to the sometimes less well-informed current affairs programmes which are wholly separate from the news, and not always on either of the two main channels.

PERSPECTIVES AND PRIORITIES

Take another kind of situation which will illustrate the point. Suppose a politician is making a speech and that there is a fracas or physical disturbance at his meeting. The odds are that television coverage will pick out the fracas, if it is violent and visual enough, at the expense of what is said in the speech. It is true that the circumstances of the violent disturbance may sometimes be more significant than the familiar arguments of the speech. But television's tendency to emphasize 'the happening' is dangerous in three respects: first, it involves a news-value judgment which obscures or belittles the reasoned argument; second, it may have ignored the possibility that by showing the fracas, television is magnifying the importance of something it may itself have created, because the fracas may have been inspired by the presence of TV cameras; third, it has the effect of putting television at the disposal of those whose aim it is to wreck, rather than to reason. Television news, unless it is transformed, will continue to lack journalistic perspective. In short: the 'hot' stuff will usually tend to squeeze out the 'cool' stuff.

When you said that certain elements will be 'lacking', did you mean that they will not figure at all, if the present type of television news programme continues?

No. They will not be lacking completely. There are traces of these elements in television news as it is. There is some interviewing, some interpretation and some expert analysis. But not enough. It was encouraging to see BBC 2's *News Extra* moving in the direction which I am advocating. But according to press reports, *News Extra* will have been cut back by the time this book is published.

In BBC2's *Newsday*, which was launched under its able producer Christopher Capron in September 1974, we broke new ground by combining in one fifteen-minute programme a brief news summary with an interview or discussion as close to the main news topics as could be arranged. *Newsday* demonstrated, and went some way to meet, the need for longer interview-discussion items dealing with the news. That need is not adequately met either in the main news programmes, or in the current affairs programmes. The longer news interview or discussion is an important feature of TV journalism which should be regularly incorporated in an expanded and transformed TV news—not relegated to the mini-minority audience which turns on BBC 2 at the opening of its transmission at 7.30 p.m.

There are some good film reports in the present TV news programmes. ITN, for instance, has commendably tried to solve the time-problem by presenting a series of special film reports in the present news programmes on successive nights from one place, as with reports on Rhodesia by Michael Nicholson in 1974. On major news occasions, when one story dominates the news (e.g. the Middle East war) both news services expand their length and improve the explanatory element considerably.

THE CURRENT AFFAIRS DIMENSION

But are not these deficiencies in television news made up in the many 'current affairs' programmes—Nationwide, Newsday, Panorama, This Week, Today, Midweek (or its replacement) and so on ad infinitum, or should I say ad nauseam?
The deficiencies are made up only in the sense that these other programmes are also part of television's general output. The deficiencies are not made up within the prime area of television journalism, namely the main news programmes on the mass audience channels.

Nonetheless these other programmes are there on the screen. Do they not redress the balance to a great extent?
No. Only to a limited extent, and in a limited way. Not only because current affairs programmes are separate from the main news output, but because they do not, on a consistent and regular basis, make up all the news deficiencies. The two elements—news and current affairs— are different only in name. They should be integrated. We need them in juxtaposition.

Current affairs programmes do not necessarily include items which serve as adequate explanatory background to the news. On some evenings there is no 'current affairs' item at all on an important news story of the day. All these programmes include interesting items of varying degrees of topicality and importance, but they do not consistently provide that additional dimension to the news which is required.

Even when the current affairs programmes bear directly on the news they tend to suffer from two shortcomings. First: they do not always include an adequate, balanced and factual introduction. By being separate from the news they sometimes lack that essential element. Second: the journalistic knowledge and experience of those dealing with some of the current affairs programmes is not always as expert as that of those on news programmes.

My argument boils down to this: that the main television news, professional though it is within its present limits, requires an extra dimension. That means a transformation of the present news programmes into something which is longer, deeper and more comprehensive.

The present news programmes on the two main channels are bedevilled with the old-fashioned concept of the news 'bulletin'. The journalistic output of television is bedevilled with the old-fashioned but still-prevailing distinction between 'news' and 'current affairs'. 'News' on television cannot achieve its full potential as a balanced service unless 'news' is understood to include what all newspapers, and radio programmes like *The World at One* include, namely the additional news dimension which is now supposed to be provided by 'current affairs'.

THE HOUR OF NEWS

This means that the main television news should be expanded to an hour in length, and transformed into something with depth and variety, i.e. a newspaper of the screen. I have no doubt that 'The Hour of News' should be the next big step forward in television journalism, the biggest since ITN launched *News at Ten* as a half-hour programme in 1967. *News at Ten*'s tremendous popular and professional success has been a resounding defeat for those who so contemptuously predicted that the mass audience would not stand for half an hour of news.

But *News at Ten* has not entirely lived up to some of the ideas which inspired its creation. It was intended to be more than a longer 'bulletin' and to include some element of what is called 'current affairs'. It would be unfair to suggest that *News at Ten* has merely achieved news at length instead of news in depth. But they have not gone as far in the latter direction as might have been hoped, especially in view of ITN's own ventures with the wider current affairs dimension, such as *Roving Report* and *Dateline*, which disappeared when *News at Ten* began.

(*Left*) 2nd Lieutenant RA, 1944 and (*right*) with Geoffrey Johnson Smith during their Oxford Union debating tour of American Universities in 1949

President of the Oxford Union, with Randolph Churchill and Professor C. E. M. Joad, in 1950

(*Left*) ITN Reporter on the Suez Canal, 1956

(*Below*) ITN interview with President Nasser in Cairo, 1957

One explanation is that for a TV news programme, twenty-five or thirty minutes (once thought to be intolerably long) has now been found to be a roughly natural length, and can be amply filled by basic news items. The added dimension which is now needed can only be achieved with extra time.

Do you really think the public want a whole hour of news?
Those who opposed half an hour for *News at Ten* thought they knew what 'the public' wanted. It is arrogant and patronizing for anyone to say they know what the public want. The public is a vast collection of very different individuals and kinds of individual, living in very different conditions and places. Our duty in television is to learn what the public appear to appreciate or not, when they have been offered it. A decision as to what to offer them requires courage, imagination and respect—respect for the viewing public. If you do not treat them with respect they, in the end, will not respect you.

That is all very well, but in suggesting that the viewers should be offered a whole hour of news, you must have reasons for expecting (as opposed to knowing) that they will like it. What are those reasons?
My main reason is that it would not be a whole hour of news in the present form. It would be quite different. It would be both deeper and more varied, with many new ingredients scarcely if ever touched by television news now. Apart from the extra depth (the explanatory and probing elements I have mentioned) it would include a whole new range of coverage. There would be feature stories arising out of all kinds of topical subjects—and not merely political and 'hard' news subjects. One of the greatest gaps in television news is the omission of many human interest stories of the sort which give colour and humour and gaiety to the newspapers.

But would these not lead to a lot more triviality of the kind you have been inveighing against?
Triviality does not arise from the subject but from the way it is treated. A three-minute film story about some simple human incident or problem may, if it is done with sensitivity or humour, and without intrusion into privacy, be infinitely less trivial and objectionable than a twenty-minute item on a heavy political subject which is treated ignorantly and superficially. What is more, an unpretentious story

about an unknown person and their family would often help to redress the balance of television news in favour of reasonable normality.
News need not be all disasters and conflict and violence. It is certainly
not so in the newspapers. Television news seems almost to have
forgotten about the news which comes out of normal life. The shortcomings of television news in this respect may be seen in the fact that
when it does cover a human story of the kind I have mentioned, that
story is invariably done as a follow-up to the newspapers which show
more imagination and initiative.

*What about the argument that news is what it is, because no one goes
out to look at their neighbour's house unless it is on fire?*
That, if I may say so, is one of those silly stock arguments which
totally miss the point. I am not suggesting that news in any media
should be artificially forced to include a lot of dull things which have
no interest whatsoever. But you only have to look at the newspapers
for it to be proved, if proof be needed, that there is news in humanity,
in humour, in eccentricity, in charity, in courage, and in

'That best portion of a good man's life,
His little, nameless, unremembered acts
Of kindness and of love.'

A NEWSPAPER OF THE SCREEN

So don't tell me that a newspaper of the screen could not include, without striving artificially, an enormous range of stories which would
justify their inclusion, not by importance, not by being sensational, not
by bloodiness, but by their warmth, their humour and their unaffected
simplicity. We have more than enough 'hard' news. There is surely
room for some soft news as well.

There are many areas in which a transformed television news could
usefully introduce expanded coverage—in 'specialist' areas such as
sport, industry, the City, education, science, books, the arts, and of
course showbusiness. These are given full and lively treatment in
newspapers. Their regular inclusion in the transformed television
news would greatly widen its appeal and interest. In all these areas

there are issues, events, and personalities to be presented in a way which television news cannot do adequately at present.

With particular reference to one important area, it would be necessary to improve on television's coverage of business and industry in current affairs programmes. This is often thought by businessmen to show anti-capitalist and left-wing bias, and by trade unionists to show an anti-trade union bias. My own opinion is that the inadequacies in TV's coverage of business and industry should be attributed less to bias or motivation of that kind than to another factor. Most people involved in television programme-making have had their education, training and professional experience in the intellectual and journalistic worlds of ideas, words, principles and the illustration thereof. They have had little or no experience of the world of action, decisions, enterprise, organization, management, negotiation and risk-taking. This leads to a lack of understanding and sympathy which must be remedied by bringing into television more people who (as on many newspapers) have some specialized knowledge and experience of business, industry and commerce. If there were in television as many such specialists as there are specialists in (say) sport, politics, foreign affairs and emotive social problems like drug-taking, our TV coverage would be much improved. TV news which is expanded into a newspaper of the screen would need to include extremely well-informed coverage of business and industry. Such coverage would have to be built up from the specialist knowledge which already exists, but can only be inadequately used, in the present TV news services.

A most important new element would be recorded extracts from the televising of Parliament, which should not be far off. Even in an expanded TV news, these would be limited to the main points from statements, speeches and exchanges. They could be better handled with more time than is available within the present news time limits. I am not referring here to a television version of *To-day in Parliament*. That would be a separate and self-contained programme.

In expanding and transforming the news to include all the various other elements how would you safeguard the purity and objectivity of 'The News'? How would you prevent 'The News' from being contaminated by the current affairs dimension you wish to add?
I wish this point could sometimes be discussed without using tendentious words like 'purity' and 'contaminated'. I am not suggesting any

lowering of news standards of accuracy and fairness. I am asking that those same standards be applied with greater depth and explanation, and with a greater variety of topics. Insofar as the 'hot' and tabloid character of television's news would be balanced by more 'cool' and considered material, this would be a raising of standards.

THE PURITY OF THE NEWS

As to the 'purity' of 'The News', this must be seen in the perspective of television history, particularly in the BBC. Let us consider 'The News', which it is now said might be contaminated by being broadened out into a wider concept of news. The present version of 'The News' is totally different from what was regarded as 'The News' on television twenty years ago. Yet despite the many changes in style and presentation, 'The News' today is regarded as still having such a great purity and objectivity as to need safeguarding. The simple fact is that the accuracy and objectivity of the news is still a basic principle and has not been weakened by changing methods of applying it.

Don't forget that something on the lines I have suggested has already been a great success on BBC radio. *The World at One* and *The World this Week-end*, combine news—pure as pure can be—with 'current affairs' which in these programmes provides news analysis and news interviews on a refreshing range of topics. Mr William Hardcastle and his producer, Mr Andrew Boyle, have established a landmark in the history of broadcast journalism by adding that dimension to the news.

> *Would not your 'transformation' affect the news standards, because the extra production staff and reporters who would have to be brought in from what is now 'current affairs', and who, according to you, may not all be as expert as the news people ?*

I would not dream of suggesting the transformation if this was a danger. Obviously nobody would be brought in unless their work had already shown the standards required. Even now there are 'current affairs' reporters (of whom I am one) whose interviews and reports have been used in 'The News' on important occasions. So far as I am aware, the 'purity' of 'The News' has not been contaminated thereby.

During the 1970 election there was a joint operation in the BBC between news and current affairs, all working in the same huge studio, to cover the campaign. There were television journalists from two separate departments, with supposedly different traditions of work and supposedly different standards. But they all welded together, each gaining from each other's professional approach. Standards of truth and fairness were upheld to the highest degree. If that can be achieved in a general election campaign, which for television is always a mine-field, it can surely be done at other times.

Do you think there is any serious chance of your 'Hour of News' coming into operation?

Oh yes. I'm certain it will come in some form, similar to what I have suggested. The case for it is overwhelming. It may be ignored or bitterly opposed for some time. Don't expect it too quickly. Look at all those ideas which we now think are obvious, and which took so long to get accepted. So with the 'Hour of News'. It will come.

I think there is now a growing feeling that the balance in television journalism should be redressed in favour of reason and understanding, with the aim of counteracting those tendencies inherent in this visual medium to over-emphasize the sensational and the violent, tendencies against which I sounded a warning (in my *Encounter* article) five years ago. I have been interested to note that other and younger television journalists have come to echo this concern, from their own experience. For instance Mr John Birt of London Weekend Television has written: 'There is a bias in television journalism. It is not against any particular party or point of view. It is a bias against understanding.'[1]

But there may be less agreement on the remedy than on the diagnosis. One proposal attributed to Mr Birt, in collaboration with Mr Peter Jay, is that television news should be reduced and even further condensed into a few minutes, and that there should then be longer treatment of the main items by way of news analysis and explanation. Such a proposal is significantly different from mine, which is that television news should be lengthened, deepened and changed in character, so as to include the analysis and explanation in which it is at present too deficient. I want to ensure that the extra dimension of news analysis, the probing and discussion (known now as 'current affairs'), is integrated with and built into the news programme

[1]Article in *The Times*, February 28th 1975.

and there handled in accordance with the highest standards of accuracy and impartiality. Otherwise there would be a danger that the rules of accuracy and impartiality would apply only to the shortened and condensed news, while the longer and subsequent news analysis could (though I do not suggest that this is the Jay/Birt intention) become a vehicle for tendentious, opinionated, and biased coverage of issues.

8. Politics and the Box

In view of your concern that TV should uphold the democratic process, do you feel some sense of guilt, in that television may have debased the currency of political debate, and made politics into a battle between personalities who must be able to 'come across on the telly'?

I have asked myself this question many times. I have worried about it until my conclusions are very confused. My first instinct is to say that television has not put a premium on personality, and has not polarized politics and elections into gladiatorial shows and personality duels between two tele-leaders. I say this because these things existed long before television was ever heard of. If we look back to over a hundred years ago, British politics was dominated by Gladstone and Disraeli ,with their deeply contrasting styles and characters. Both were much more striking, more legendary and more hypnotic personalities (in the true sense of that debased word) than any of our contemporary figures would claim to be. If I may quote from Robert Blake's *Disraeli*: 'They polarized political opinion.' Lord Blake refers to 'the great parliamentary duel which for twenty-eight years was to be a feature of English public life and to dominate it for the last twelve of them. . . . As time went on the two men came to embody in the eyes of the nation the opposing elements in politics and to personify according to the prejudices of the onlooker the forces of good and evil.'[1]

So the kind of politics which centres on the conflict of leader-personalities can hardly be said to have been originated by television.

But that is not quite the point, which is: has not television, by its own pressures and techniques put a premium on shoddy political communication which is on a much lower level than that of your two Great Victorians? Has not television debased the requirements of political leadership by forcing politicians into fireside chattiness, ad-man language, bedside

[1]*Disraeli*, by Robert Blake, p. 346.

Harold Wilson.

Edward Heath.

'I thought they weren't allowing no more political satire until after the election.'

manners, quick-fire responses to loaded questions, and a slick friendliness more suitable to selling soap than leading a nation?

If any politician today imagines that the way to 'come across' on television is to use that sort of shoddy nonsense, then he sadly underestimates the electorate. The people are not such fools, But I take the point. Politicians today, with a very few exceptions, do not speak with much nobility of language or grandeur of style. That is due to the general change in political style which was not wholly caused by television. Most of our leading politicians, such as Mr Wilson, speak in a style which is more in tune with a less aristocratic kind of politics and with the unromantic problems of our time.

It is not the most natural thing to speak in heroic phrases about the re-cycling of the oil revenues, or to use the language of Macaulay in discussing the money supply. The metaphors of the football field are preferred to those of the battlefield. The cultural allusions are to Mike Yarwood or Ken Dodd rather than to Virgil or Horace. Each of us will have our own view as to whether this should be regretted as a lowering of political communication to television's level, or welcomed as making it more meaningful to ordinary people in the age of mass-democracy. In any event political communication in this country is still more articulate and eloquent than in certain other democracies which come to mind.

It is interesting to consider those few politicians who still go in for rhetoric in the grand manner, and for the style and eloquence of language associated with Parliaments of the past, such as Enoch Powell, Roy Jenkins, Lord Hailsham and Michael Foot (who though a master of the crudest style of Party Conference harangue, can be an orator of great eloquence). The significant thing is that all these gentlemen, despite the allegedly degrading requirements of television, are notable 'performers on the box'. They do not make intellectual or linguistic concessions to their audience, and do not go in for the cosy bedside manner. So although television may have encouraged *some* politicians to adopt the chatty style, it has not forced all of them into that mould. Indeed all politicians and public figures would be well advised to ignore any advice they may be given by the TV 'training schools' as to what television requires. They should speak on television in the style which is their own. That is what will come across if they are men of any quality.

TELEVISION AND THE DOWNFALL OF MR HEATH

Nonetheless is there not a tendency for television to impose its values on the qualities required for leadership? Could it not be argued that Mr Edward Heath, regarded even by his opponents as a statesman of serious purpose and high ability, came to his political downfall because he lacked or refused to cultivate the kind of showbiz personality which comes across on the telly?

I don't accept that view, though it is quite commonly held. For one thing, the Edward Heath who lost the two elections of 1974 was the same Edward Heath who won the election of 1970—against all the odds. That does not suggest that you can blame television, or its alleged personality requirements, for Mr Heath's downfall. His personal triumph in the Referendum campaign is further evidence to support this view.

You could argue that if he had been able to 'come across' better on television he might have won in 1974, at least in the February election when the margin was narrow. I would doubt that however, because in the February election his television appearances were very effective. What lost him that election was not any failure to come across on television, but a series of other factors which tipped the balance in Labour's favour, such as the realization that the miners would get more money even if the Tories won, which cast doubt on the whole object of the election, the so-called 'muddle' over the miners' pay comparison figures, Campbell Adamson's remarks on the Industrial Relations Act and Enoch Powell's advice to vote Labour.

That may be your opinion, but some people will remain convinced that Mr Heath was a statesman of great stature and integrity who was kicked out by his party because he lacked the appeal required in the television age. If there is any truth in that, doesn't it mean that television is corrupting our political values?

If there was truth in that suggestion, it could be argued that television is corrupting our political values. Even if he was voted out for 'lack of appeal' this was not for lack of 'television' appeal, but because he was thought to lack certain personal qualities needed by a leader in any age. But I do not believe that Mr Heath's downfall was due to his supposed failure as a vote-winning TV personality. It may be interesting to note the considered opinion of two distinguished political analysts who write from very different political viewpoints.

Mr Ronald Butt wrote in *The Times*, after Mr Heath had lost the leadership: 'It is worth saying again that Mr Heath was not defeated because he did not do well on television, or even because he had lost two general elections. He was overthrown because he had lost two general elections in support of policies which his party did not in its heart believe and which it only reluctantly accepted.'[1] Mr Peter Jenkins in the *Guardian* reached a similar conclusion on the first point, but puts the explanation differently: 'The fatal complaint against Mr Edward Heath was not so much his alleged inability to win votes, but that having won power he failed to exercise it successfully and in the end cast it away.'[2]

Even if you think Mr Heath's downfall was not due to television's personality requirements, are you completely convinced that television is not tending to debase the quality of political leadership in any way?

No. I am not convinced. I am still confused. Television, as the main mass medium of news and opinion, is bound to have some effect on the choice of political leaders and on the way they communicate with the electorate. I am not convinced that this influence will be such as to raise the level of political debate and the quality of political leadership.

Success on television is no indication of the greatest human qualities and may easily be achieved by fifth-rate people. Sometimes I am tempted to think that television (as Francis Bacon said of fame) 'is like a river, that beareth up things light and swollen, and drowns things weighty and solid'.

THE CAMERAS AND THE COMMONS

Do not your doubts on this question tell against your own case for televising Parliament, on the grounds that the television cameras might well cause lowering of the level there and an over-emphasis on things (or MPs) 'light and swollen'?

No. The televising of Parliament would be an entirely different situation from that which prevails in a TV studio. This is one of the points on which there is most misunderstanding. In the televising of Parliament, the TV cameras would be visitors to cover a public event,

[1] *The Times*, February 13th 1975.
[2] The *Guardian*, February 7th 1975.

'*Daddy thinks I'll ask simpler questions.*'

as it happens and in the way it happens; and Parliament has its own long-established style and standards. In a TV studio the parliamentarians come to the TV cameras, for a TV production with television's style and standards. And they may adapt to what they think is necessary for television. The televising of Parliament would not be the creation of a producer, it would be a public event to be faithfully reported by the camera and microphone.

Are you saying that the style and standards of Parliament would not be changed at all?

I think the only way it might change (though after a short time no one would be too conscious of the cameras) would be that certain kinds of behaviour which are not in the finest Parliamentary tradition would be found objectionable to the viewing electorate. For instance not long ago I saw an MP make a physical gesture which would not have impressed a great many people including some of his loyal constituents. The MP in question was being subjected to some interrruption. His response was to lift up his right leg, and to thrust out his groin at his interrupters, in the manner of a dog urinating at a lamp-post. The gesture was clear and unmistakable. If the television cameras had been present to show that gesture, they would have been blamed for it. But of course if television cameras had been present, the gesture would probably not have been made. And if such a gesture (trivial admittedly but rather squalid) were to be seen on television there would surely be a sharp reaction. Not that people are particularly genteel, but they have a reasonable (with apologies for coming back to that word) sense of what is fitting.

TV AND THE RADIO REVIVAL

During the last five of your twenty years in television you have also done a lot of radio. What is your comment on a recent statement by the Labour MP Mr Raymond Fletcher: 'Sound broadcasting is coming back and becoming the proper medium for political discourse with our electors. Take my tip, brothers: five minutes on The World at One *will do your good causes much more good these days than half-an-hour with either Michael Parkinson or Russell Harty.'?*[1]

[1] *The Listener*, February 13th 1975.

Shortly after Mr Fletcher made that comment the House of Commons voted by a massive majority for an experiment in the radio broadcasting of Parliament, but against television by a few votes. So radio does appear to be respected more and suspected less by politicians. But Mr Fletcher was wrong to say: 'Sound broadcasting is coming back.' Radio *is* back, and has been back for several years. Late as Mr Fletcher was in saluting radio's revival, there is a lot in his point; except that I did not realize that Messrs Parkinson and Harty offered many opportunities for active politicians. Nor would I approve of it if they did.

Politicians' access to television's powerful platform should be at the reasonable price of critical and informed examination of their views. They should not be encouraged to use it as an easy means of personality projection, like film-stars who want to plug their new film.

As to radio's advantages, there is no doubt that many politicians are tending to think of television for exposure, and radio for exposition. But despite the great merits of radio, politicians would be wrong to treat television too contemptuously. As I have been trying to argue, television need not be used only for visual effect. It *can* be used for intelligent communication. Politicians and others might be surprised how many viewers will appreciate being treated with respect.

One reason for BBC Radio's revival has been the imaginative development of news and news analysis programmes such as *The World at One*. After being pushed into the shade by television's upsurge in the 'fifties and 'sixties, BBC Radio recovered confidence, and developed a new vigour. The Commons' vote in 1975 to choose radio for the first historic experiment in the broadcasting of Parliament is certain to have proved a major advance for the medium which no one calls 'steam' any more.

In the last two elections some of the most effective and newsworthy programmes were on radio. The morning *Election Call*, in which listeners telephoned their questions directly to leading politicians, was a landmark in democratic communication. In David Butler's book on the General Election of February 1974, *Election Call* is described as 'the great success' of broadcasting in that campaign: 'Clearly a new campaign tradition had been born.' The success of *Election Call* (due to the freshness and force of the callers' questions) grew out of *It's Your Line*, which precipitated a multiplicity of 'phone-in' programmes of varying quality.

9. 'Don't Muck About With the BBC'

The future of both television and radio is being considered by the Annan Committee. What advice would you offer after your twenty years experience?
My advice, or rather my humble plea, would be very simple: Don't muck about with the BBC.

Is that all?
No, but it is fundamental. Leave the BBC alone. Criticize it, probe it, suggest improvements to it—but leave it alone. By that I mean: do not impair that constitutional position which has fostered the development of its independence and excellence for more than half a century. If any change in the BBC's position is considered it should be only in the direction of reinforcing its constitutional and financial independence.

How is that advice consistent with some of your critical observations in this dialogue?
Most of my criticisms and anxieties have been about television as a medium. In so far as my criticisms relate to the BBC, that is a tribute to the high standards which the BBC has always set itself. If the day ever came that no one criticized the BBC, whether from inside or outside, it would be because the BBC was no longer worth criticizing.

Any criticisms which can be made of the BBC must be seen in the perspective of its overall achievement, In an age when this country has suffered many blows to its self-confidence, the BBC has remained one of our greatest national assets, in which pride can be taken. Whatever its faults, it is an unrivalled example to the world of independence and excellence in broadcasting.

May not that assertion, unless supported by evidence, be dismissed as mere chauvinism?
To hell with whether anyone calls it chauvinistic, but there is abundant

evidence to justify it: the evidence of countless visitors to this country and of residents here from abroad. It is true that only a small proportion of the world's nations can be called anything like free or democratic, so the scope for relevant comparison is limited. In case there should be any doubt in anyone's mind of the widespread respect in which the BBC is held, the Annan Committee, whose travels may not be extensive enough for this purpose, could arrange for a survey of opinion among foreign and Commonwealth residents in this country. To be fair, it should be conceded that those who come here from abroad may express commendation of 'British' television rather than of the BBC alone. I would not begrudge ITV credit for an outstanding record among commercial broadcasting systems, and ITN is a major achievement. Though the competition has worked both ways, the existence of the BBC has a good effect on ITV. That is another reason why nothing should be recommended by the Annan Committee which would interfere with or derogate from the independence and standing of the BBC.

As to evidence of the BBC's reputation, may I quote the objective verdict of the American magazine *Newsweek*, which recently did a world survey of television: 'The BBC consistently maintains the highest standards of any TV network anywhere.'[1]

We still have some things to be proud of, and that is one of them.

But even granted that the BBC is excellent compared with other broadcasting systems, is that any reason why we, the British, should be satisfied with it?

We should not be satisfied with it. The BBC is not satisfied with itself. Undoubtedly the BBC is the best, but it could be much better.

MORE ADVICE FOR ANNAN

Apart from your plea that they should 'not muck about with the BBC', what other suggestions would you offer to the Annan Committee?

First: as regards the fourth or any further TV channel, I would suggest the following points for their consideration:

1. It should not be allotted in whole or in part to any existing TV

[1]*Newsweek*, April 22nd 1974: Special issue on 'TV: The World Turns On'.

organizations. The BBC is quite big enough already. I can see the economic case for enabling the existing ITV studios and other resources to be more productively used if the fourth channel were made into an ITV 2. But I would oppose this for two reasons: First: the ITV companies have already been given a share in the very exclusive access to the profit-making opportunities of commercial television. Second: an ITV 2 would offer too great a temptation to make ITV 1 all the more mass-audience orientated with consequent temptation to BBC 1 standards. There is a danger that ITV 1 would be treated as an opportunity to slough off responsibilities for certain kinds of programme on to ITV 2.

2. The fourth or further channel should have as its main purpose the use of television for education and information (in the broadest senses) rather than entertainment.

3. It should be run on a new basis which would permit a much greater diversity of access and control despite the limitations imposed by the scarcity of public 'channels'.

This basis would be that a new Board or Authority would commission, like a publisher, a wide and balanced variety of programme-making units each of whom would have complete editorial independence for its regular programme slot, subject only to the ordinary laws of libel, etc, and free from the duty of impartiality. This idea was originally outlined in my 1961 book. It was ignored by the Pilkington Committee, but recently appears to have been broadly adopted in the proposal for a National Television Foundation. The commissioning of programmes would be done on a periodical basis in the light of standards achieved. The commissioning agency would provide studios and other technical facilities (as a publisher arranges for printing). Those commissioned to make programmes on a daily, weekly or monthly basis would receive funds for their budget. The Board or Authority would transmit but not control. It would select but not supervise. It would have no power over programme content once the choice of programme-maker is made, except the power of non-renewal. Such a system would offer opportunities for entry into television programme-making which would not be limited to rich consortia.

There could be various ways by which such a system could be financed: (i) by direct grant from Government to the Commissioning agency, on conditions of independence comparable to the financing of Universities through the UGC; (ii) by commercial advertising on the

present ITV system; (iii) by commercial sponsorship which though it
has hitherto been regarded as unthinkable in British TV, could be used
in a way which would encourage the presentation of prestige programmes. Sponsorship would be carefully regulated. Available programmes
could be offered for sponsorship under a system which would prevent a
sponsor from dictating content; (iv) by a combination of the above
three ways.

As regards ITV generally, the Annan Committee should strongly
recommend that the IBA should take a much more positive role in
influencing the balance of ITV material. This would ensure that ITV's
commercial concern for the mass-audience does not go to such lengths
as to force the BBC to lower standards.

More positive IBA intervention might redress the ITV balance of
material in favour of more serious and intelligent programmes at better
viewing times. An analytical current affairs programme like *Weekend
World* should not be thrown away at the off-peak hour of noon on
Sundays.

ENTRENCHING THE INDEPENDENCE OF THE BBC

*You mentioned the possible need to reinforce the BBC's constitutional
position. Why and in what way?*
The BBC, in law, is wholly subject to the power of Government. It
can, in law, be ordered what to broadcast, and what not to broadcast.
The Board of Governors could in law, be sacked by Government
whim. In practice, the power of Government has not been abused, and
a strong convention of independence has been established. That practical independence is said to rest on three supports: (1) the fact that if
the BBC were not seen to be independent no one would trust or believe
it; (2) the continuance of parliamentary democracy under which attempts to suppress or control the BBC would be resisted; (3) the licence
fee system, which gives it a source of revenue separate from taxation
and free from government interference as to how it is spent.

I am one of those who regard these supports for the BBC's independence as no longer strong enough whatever the practice may have
been hitherto.

We cannot tell what the future may bring. We live in an age when
conventions, and traditions of behaviour, are overturned or defied.
I therefore think there is a case for considering ways in which the

conventions on which BBC independence rests could be reinforced by something stronger. There are several methods of constitutional reinforcement which could be considered. In particular there could be a broadcasting Bill of Rights to entrench the BBC's position. This statute could include certain provisions which would give the BBC a position of constitutional independence comparable to but not identical with that of the higher judiciary. One provision of such a statute would be designed to safeguard the licence-fee system—which is the most vulnerable of those supports on which BBC independence rests. The Annan Committee should study how such a safeguard could be written into a new statute. It would be important that this should (i) safeguard the licence-fee system (ii) guarantee the BBC a right to the full licence revenue and (iii) safeguard the amount of the licence-fee in real terms by providing for some system of indexation to the rate of inflation.

The statute could include a provision that no Government order to the BBC should be issued without the consent of both Houses of Parliament on a procedure which required notice and debate.

Another provision might provide that the BBC Governors could not be removed except by a similar procedure in Parliament. If the Annan Committee were to make careful inquiries they might come to the conclusion that the danger of a Government seeking to remove the Board of Governors has not always been so remote from reality.

A further provision might be that the Chairman and Governors of the BBC would be appointed not, as at present, by the Crown on the advice of the Prime Minister or the Minister responsible for Broadcasting, but by the Crown on advice tendered by a new system. The Crown would be advised on such appointments by a Committee of HM Privy Council consisting of the Prime Minister, the Leader of the Opposition and one non-political Privy Councillor of high standing and distinction. The third man (or woman) would be chosen by the agreement of both the other two. Advice to the Crown would have to be unanimous. Such a system would not entirely destroy the Prime Minister's traditional patronage in this matter. No doubt his nominee would normally be accepted, particularly under a system which deterred obviously unacceptable choices. The new system would be a useful check against appointments which might be seen as capricious, vindictive, nepotistic or aimed at weakening the BBC's independence.

The safeguards relating to the removal of, and appointment to, the BBC Board of Governors, and to the Government's power to issue instructions, could be extended to the IBA.

The normal tenure of office of the Chairman of the BBC and the IBA could be lengthened to seven years. This would help to strengthen their moral authority in the Government's eyes and in those of their professional executives.

Are not such ideas for constitutional safeguards open to the criticism that if we have got to a stage when a Government is so evilly disposed and ruthless as to crush the BBC, it will ignore or get round any constitutional or parliamentary safeguard?

This is the orthodox argument. In an extreme situation nothing would be safe. But nations do not necessarily plunge into despotism overnight. There may be gradual progress towards that end, by salami tactics or pin-pricks rather than the sudden bludgeon of full-scale repression. There could be great restraining value in new constitutional protections (not admittedly if the tanks were outside Broadcasting House) which would be there to make a Government pause. To say that safeguards enshrined in statute are no use because a really ruthless Government could sweep them away, is to say that Habeas Corpus is no use, or that the constitutional procedure required for the removal of a High Court Judge is no use.

The ideas which I have put forward in this area involve difficult problems of constitutional law and procedure An individual offering advice to the Annan Committee can do no more than to put them forward in principle. Detailed consideration and drafting would be a matter for an expert study which the Annan Committee should, in my respectful submission, arrange. Whatever may be wrong with my particular suggestions, I am convinced that there should be no risks taken with the future independence of the BBC. There are those who do not value it greatly.

THE LIE OF THE IMAGE

Finally: is there anything that you have really detested about your twenty years in television?

No question about it: that which is known as my 'image'. Some people are thought to be so very pleasant and charming when they are in fact such nasty pieces of work. And I, who am as you have found the most good-natured of men, bubbling with fun, am thought to be a thoroughly objectionable fellow. That's what television does for you.

Being aware of that image, do you have some sympathy for those who have had to watch you for the last twenty years?
I do indeed. Heartfelt. But they haven't *had* to watch.

Mr Day, thank you.
Thank you, Robin.

PART II

Troubled Reflections of a TV Journalist

Troubled Reflections of a TV Journalist[1]

So swift and dramatic has been television's growth that the full consequences of its impact on human life and affairs are not yet clearly discernible. The speed of its development, social and technological, has been fantastic. It has spread to the poor countries of the third world. In affluent societies it is in almost every home. Satellites orbiting in space transmit events in one part of this planet to another; a landing by man on the moon has been seen by men everywhere on earth. Colour television makes monochrome look as old-fashioned as radio seemed at the beginning of television.

The fifteen years which I have spent as a television journalist have coincided with the years in which television has expanded into a world phenomenon. As a journalist of the new electronic medium, I have reported events and issues in the variety of forms which television journalism has developed—newscasting; verbal reporting to camera; descriptive comment on events televised as they happen; presenting studio programmes on topical issues; making films; writing commentary for film reports and documentaries; and interviewing—this being a function which in British television has been developed into a new instrument of journalistic inquiry and a controversial feature of the political scene.

None of this makes one better qualified than any other citizen to pass opinion or moral judgment about television's effect on society. But professional involvement in the television coverage of events during the last decade and a half enables me to illustrate the difficulties and dangers of television as a journalistic medium and to suggest how these may be overcome.

Television journalists (editors, producers, reporters) find that in trying to make the best use of their potent medium, they have to grapple with the extremely challenging limitations which affect television as a medium of journalistic communication. These limitations are of two kinds: imposed and inherent—those which arise from the

[1]Originally published in *Encounter*, May 1970.

system under which television is allowed to operate, and those which arise from the very nature of the medium itself.

The imposed limitations are the most obvious—control, interference and pressure from governments and politicians; and control, interference and pressure from commercial interests, i.e. advertisers, who may be involved in certain television systems. The dangers of these pressures are greatly increasing. As the technology of television (video-tape, satellites, colour) develops, television is becoming more and more expensive. That means that those responsible for television, especially on the journalistic side, become more and more dependent on either politicians or commercial interests for their money.

The degree to which television suffers from control and pressure is, of course, a reflection of the society in which it operates. Television is simply an instrument of communication, which can be used for good or evil. Arsenic can be used as a weed-killer or as a wife-killer. So can television be used as an instrument of tyranny and propaganda, or as an instrument of democratic liberties and critical discussion. Even under a free democratic system, such as in Britain, television has imposed on it a fundamental limitation—the duty to be impartial and accurate in its coverage of news and events. That duty means that an impartial television service (unlike the press) cannot propagandize its own opinions. It must, broadly speaking, present 'both sides' of every question. This principle is not always easy to apply in practice, especially when a question has more than two sides, or when a question has, in the overwhelming opinion of the moment, only one side.

So in a democratic country where the TV services are enjoined to be impartial, the television journalist is basically confined to two functions: (1) reporting, investigating and analysing facts, and (2) presenting and examining the opinions of others.

Though he is denied the right to propagate his own opinions he still has (or should have) one of the ancient weapons of journalism in his hands: the right to ask questions, the right to probe and inquire. He is not, as campaigning newspaper men sometimes suggest, a 'castrated journalist'. Television need not become a handy instrument of mass hypnosis for politicians and others in authority, if TV journalists use their right to inquire with vigour and persistence, The right to enquire is enhanced, not limited, by the duty of impartiality.

One reason why television may have imposed on it a duty of impartiality is that whereas you need have no limit on the number of printing presses, there are a limited number of TV channels available. In order to operate, a TV service has to be granted the right to use what is part of a scarce public asset. This is what differentiates TV (and radio) from other media—press, cinema, books, theatre—which do not (or should not) require any such permission from a Government, and do not depend on the state for their method of communication with the people.

This technical limitation on the number of TV outlets, however, may be overcome to some degree. Advances with the use of frequencies and transmission by cable are making possible a much larger number of TV output channels in a given area. This could be used, if there is sufficient wisdom and imagination to do so, to enable television to operate with a greater diversity of control, and, in areas served by only one or two newspapers, with a greater diversity of opinion than is available from the press. Where a country can develop a large number of TV stations serving local communities, there is great value in the American practice of local stations being licensed to transmit their own editorial opinions, labelled as such.

Those then are the *imposed* limitations on television, which vary from country to country according to the philosophy of Government.

The less obvious and more interesting limitations are those which are inherent in the medium itself. They raise fascinating and sophisticated questions regarding the philosophy of communication.

The first *inherent* limitation of television as an influence on opinion and events is that it depends on pictures. This is not intended as a very profound or original observation—but it leads to some interesting thoughts. Human communication seems to be turning full-circle back to its primitive origins. In the dim dark ages, man communicated with man by the language of pictures and visible gesture. Then came the spoken word and the written word; later still the printed word. Five hundred years after that the broadcast word through the miracle of radio; then television, first in black-and-white, and now, increasingly, in 'living colour'. Admittedly the modern picture language of television can be accompanied by words. But there is no doubt that as modern communication has become more technically advanced in method it has declined in intellectual quality and rational content.

Broadcasting in sound or vision will not, I think, prove to have contributed to the advancement of ideas or the education of man as much as the printed word. Television has proved a less serious, less intelligent, medium than radio. Colour television, by emphasizing the image even more vividly than monochrome, takes the backward process a stage further. The marvels of communication in the electronic age are taking us back to the primitive picture language of the stone age.

I do not wish to exaggerate this, but the fact is that television's dependence on pictures (and the most vivid pictures) makes it not only a *powerful* means of communication, but a *crude* one which tends to strike at the emotions rather than at the intellect. For TV journalism this means a dangerous and increasing concentration on action (usually violent and bloody) rather than on thought, on happenings rather than issues, on shock rather than explanation, in personalities rather than ideas.

TALES OF TALKING HEADS

What does this lead to in the practice of television journalism? It means that TV can cover a riot, a war, a revolution, an assassination, more vividly than any newspaper. It also means that television tends to give much less impressive treatment of the reasons behind those events. In the case of events or issues which do not have convenient visual existence, television tends to treat them inadequately. Take a key issue such as the political implications for Britain of signing the Treaty of Rome. This is hard to deal with on television except by what TV professionals tend to regard as a second-hand and second-class way—by people discussing it. Television men have a revealing phrase for this. They do not call it 'argument' or 'the exchange of ideas'; they call it 'talking heads'. In that contemptuous phrase, the image merchants of the electronic age dismiss the one characteristic of man that elevates him above the beast, the power to conceive and communicate rational thought. Man's supreme gift is seen in terms of what the eye sees on that wretched little screen: 'a talking head'.

Does this suggest that I am extremely cynical about my own profession, or that I am trying to unburden myself of an appalling guilt complex? All I am really trying to do is to point out some of the basic shortcomings and dangers of television so that we may seek ways of correcting or preventing them.

One way that we can prevent pictures from distorting or completely dominating television as a medium of information is by accompanying the pictures with words. This can, and should be done so as to give the pictures meaning and perspective. But words on television have their own limitation. They tend to be put into the background by the pictures, especially if these are extremely dramatic. And broadcast words cannot be re-heard as the printed word can be re-read if the reader so chooses. The vivid impact of the picture remains in the consciousness longer than the words of interpretation or qualification. The sight on a TV screen of a person being brutally injured will linger in the emotions far longer than the accompanying words, which pointed out that only one person out of a crowd of several hundred was assaulted and that the rest of the city was completely calm. It scarcely needs to be mentioned that pictures showing the rest of the city being completely calm would not rate as 'good television'—another piece of jargon.

There is a fascinating piece of expert evidence as to how television can cause distortion even in the most distinguished programme, and remorse even in the most distinguished commentator. In the foreword to the book[1] of his celebrated BBC series *Civilization*, Sir Kenneth (now Lord) Clark refers regretfully to the 'limitations imposed on me by the medium' and writes:

'A line of argument determined almost entirely by visual evidence does not make for logic or completeness; and in the programmes it led to a number of omissions of which I am ashamed. Even the most rapid survey of civilization should have said more than I have done about law and philosophy. *I could not think of any way of making them visually interesting.* [My italics.—R.D.] This defect is particularly serious in my treatment of Germany. I talk a lot about Bavarian Rococo and hardly mention Kant and Hegel. Goethe, who should have been one of the chief heroes of the series, makes only a brief appearance, and the German romantics are left out altogether . . .'

Out went Kant and Goethe, law and philosophy! Here, on the most elevated heights yet scaled by television, is a rarefied example of the problem so often experienced on the humbler level of news gathering.

Journalistic evaluation can be injected into the visual content of a television report. That is when the picture is not merely a silent picture backed by explanatory words but is a picture synchronised with speech.

[1]Published by John Murray and the BBC.

In that way—by a reporter's critical question, by the clash of argument —meaning and evaluation can be combined effectively with visual impact. The interpretive function is then an integral part of the visual impression. In these situations the words or expressions of an individual can have a significant and lasting impact. One simple question answered evasively or movingly or angrily can put a visual sequence into new perspective.

Some pictures need no words, no questions, no reporter. But the most vivid picture can distort the reality it appears to show unless it is combined with inquiry or explanation. Conversely, pictures can be honestly shot and dishonestly presented—with words which falsify the picture. That merely reminds us of the obvious but vital truth that the way television is used, as with any other instrument, depends in the end on the integrity and motives of those responsible for it.

The insatiable appetite of television for vivid, action-packed pictures has wide and profound implications. It means that television has a built-in tendency to present issues solely or mainly in terms of their immediately visible results. Wars on television are seen almost exclusively in terms of casualties and combat, as in the case of Vietnam, the first television war. Or as in the Biafran rebellion, in terms of starving children who were seen with sickening regularity on our television screens.

What is wrong with that? Is not starvation to be reported by showing the people who are starving? What *is* war but casualties and combat, blood and brutality? Fair enough—but television is liable to concentrate on these things to the exclusion of the ideas and issues which bring wars about. Television does not always take sufficient trouble to ask 'who is responsible', 'why is it happening', or 'what is the alternative'.

Nor is this all. Television may only be able to gather its pictures on one side of a conflict which may be equally horrifying in its cruelty on both sides. We have all seen some extremely brutal television pictures of the war in South Vietnam, most of them taken with facilities provided by the Americans. But without entering into discussion of the Vietnam issue, does anyone doubt that there are brutalities and atrocities committed in the Viet Cong-held areas? How much of that has ever been seen on television?

This leads me to another significant and rarely appreciated limitation which is inherent in television as a medium of journalism. For television to be able to cover a situation in a particular country, a number of physical requirements must be fulfilled. First, television must get in, with its elaborate equipment. That may mean a cameraman alone— but if something more serious and inquiring than crude visual journalism is intended, then it means a reporter, a sound recordist, and perhaps a producer as well. Having got in (and that is a lot less easy for a four-man television team with twenty boxes of equipment, than for a single newspaper man with one air-travel bag and a notebook) they have to be able to move about. Moving about requires capacious transport—often difficult to arrange in hostile and authoritarian countries. Moving about and setting up to film requires permission not readily granted to prying truck-loads of foreigners with their paraphernalia. Even if you get the means and the permission to move about, you then have to find people who will talk. The people whom you need to talk to may insist on not being questioned or on being questioned on certain conditions. In other words television does not get *any* report unless it can actually get the pictures it needs. In many situations television does not get adequate material unless the people who should be questioned, have been questioned on film. One further little point: even if your television team does manage to do its work it still has to get its film *out*, intact and uncensored.

So one of television's *inherent* limitations is that its coverage contains a built-in bias against free and open societies. Television is far more able to give a critical and unflattering picture of a free society than of any totalitarian one.

On the television screens of the Western world (and, no doubt, of the Communist world also) pictorial reports of violence, injustice, and protest in the United States are part of the viewers' daily diet. Much of this coverage is made and marketed throughout the world by America itself. Yet how effectively is television able to cover injustice, oppression, and brutality in other parts of the world such as China, Russia, Czechoslovakia, Spain, or Rhodesia? By reason of its own operational needs television is inherently incapable of giving fair and balanced reporting of a very large part of the world today.

It is true that newspaper reporters also have difficulty in entering and reporting from authoritarian countries. But the television journalist labours under more serious operational handicaps. He cannot wander about unobtrusively, nor produce, after leaving, a brilliant 'I Was There' story, as a newspaper reporter can. Newspapers can also publish analysis and interpretation based on expert study of publications and secret intelligence. Such deductive analysis is not convenient material for television.

This cannot fail to have a profound effect on public opinion in free countries where television is *the* mass medium of news and information. The public is constantly reminded in the most vivid way of the evils in its own society and in those other countries where television is free to prowl. But the evils of life in closed totalitarian countries cannot be given anything like the same emphasis. All of which tends to lead to a grossly distorted view of the world.

There are exceptions. One was the amazing television coverage of the Russian invasion of Czechoslovakia. But that coverage was only possible during the brief period before censorship and police state conditions were reimposed. The television coverage of Prague was only an exception to prove the rule.

More than any other medium of journalism, television is a *mass* medium. There may be minority programmes, but the main output is aimed at the mass audience. All the pressures are to present programmes with the widest possible appeal. In the century of the common man, the need for mass-appeal must be accepted—but as a challenge. Mass-appeal need *not* necessarily mean total degradation of standards or cynical contempt for the audience. Television journalism has all the great opportunities and dangerous temptations of tabloid journalism. This means, of course, the mass communication of material in highly concentrated form relying on the power of pictures backed by the clearest and fewest words possible. The opportunities of this tabloid medium are to broadcast the facts, encourage informed debate, to involve the mass of ordinary people in some understanding of the events that shape their lives. Television has these opportunities in modern society in a way that has never existed since Pericles was able to address his whole community in the *polis* of Athens.

Too often these opportunities are wasted, misused, or even ignored. Sometimes television rises to the occasion with a magnificent sense of dignity and responsibility, and the maximum use of technical potential. In the terrible days of shock and horror following the assassination of President Kennedy, television helped to unite and steady a nation at a moment of appalling tragedy. Another example is of a totally different kind which we have seen only recently—one of the climacterics of human history—the landing of the first man on the moon.

There are many other less spectacular occasions on which television

ITN Newscaster, 1957

ITN interview with Harold Macmillan, February 1958

Reporting from Red Square, February 1959

has nobly grasped its opportunities. But the tabloid vices of sensationalism and superficiality are television's constant temptation. Not only
because of the incessant pressure to be vivid and concise but because of
the technicalities of television production and presentation. This is not
the place to discuss in detail how the mechanics of getting a television
programme on the air tend to influence, sometimes to dominate, the
content, style and treatment of that programme. The simple point is
that the television journalist has to be much more conscious of his
'hardware' and 'logistics' than does the newspaper man or the radio
reporter.

Television may be the most potent medium of mass communication
the world has ever known, but because of its dangers and shortcomings those who use television as a medium of journalism are faced
with a constant challenge to their integrity and sense of responsibility.
These dangers and shortcomings may be summarised as follows:

It is a tabloid medium which deals in crude visual headlines.

It lives and thrives on pictures—above all on pictures of action.

It is better at conveying images and impressions than ideas and
intellectual arguments.

As an investigative medium it can operate very effectively in an open
democracy but much less so and often misleadingly, in an authoritarian
state.

Television's proud motto is '*see it happen*', but seeing is not necessarily
understanding and the sights selected to be seen may not be the whole
picture.

THE IRREVOCABLE COWARDICE

Against that background two main questions may be examined: (1)
What evidence is there to show how television makes its impact not
only on opinion but on events? (2) What should be done to overcome
its limitations and avoid its dangers?

Looking around the world today one can see several fascinating
examples of how television has affected the course of history.

Vietnam has been called 'the first television war'. There can be no
doubt that the effect on Americans of seeing this war (or, rather, one
side of it) in their own homes night after night had a most powerful
effect on opinion. In the past, wars were something that soldiers went

off to fight in remote places; today war is something that the people
who stay at home have to take with their supper. On the colour screens
of American homes a pool of blood is sickeningly red.

Those who take a strong view against American policy in Vietnam
will welcome the effect of television on opinion. But—detaching
ourselves from the merits of the Vietnam issue—one wonders whether
in future a democracy which has uncensored television in every home
will ever be able to fight a war, *however just.*

However good the cause—self-defence, resisting aggression, or even
fighting under the United Nations flag—the brutal details of military
action may be there on the television screen to shock and to horrify,
sapping perhaps the will of that nation to resist the forces of evil or
even to safeguard its own freedom.

When people are horrified by the sight of bloodshed and mutilation
they are not easily convinced that a cause may be at stake. The sight of
a dead child, a burning home, a dying citizen-soldier—all these may
have a much more powerful impact than abstract concepts like 'liberty'
or 'collective security'.

There may be some who may ask: if television is an ally of pacifism,
is that not hopeful for the world? The answer to that question must
depend on whether you believe in peace at any price even if that price
includes freedom or the independence of 'far-away countries of which
we know nothing . . .'.

The implications of this do not yet appear to be widely appreciated,
but the point was grasped recently in the *Economist:*

'The United States is the first country that has ever tried to fight a
televised war under the rules of democracy—free reporting, opinion
polls, the lot—and if the result has been the unsurprising discovery that
people loathe war that is something that all democracies will have to
chew over in the future.'

Americans, of course, have already begun this 'chewing over', led by
Vice-President Agnew with a mouthful of resentment against the way
the TV networks wield their power.

Unfortunately, what validity there was in Mr Agnew's criticisms
was obscured, for several reasons: the crudity of his earlier attack on the
Vietnam dissenters; the implied threat contained in his intimidating
reminder that TV stations are subject to federal licensing; his attack

on the 'small and unelected élite' of Eastern liberals, which was not merely directed at TV men but at the newspapers.

Nevertheless, however disturbing a politician Mr Agnew may be, his contention that television has helped to spread violence and extremist dissent intended to undermine the elected government cannot be brushed aside. Referring to television news, he protested (and are Vice-Presidents to be denied the right to protest?):

'Bad news drives out good. Concurrence can no longer compete with dissent. One minute of Eldridge Cleaver is worth ten minutes of Roy Wilkins.'

The networks reacted bitterly to his attacks, but (whether due to timidity, or to conscience, or to widespread public support for Mr Agnew's criticisms) they appear to have taken note.

Attempts by Administrations to manage news and to intimidate newsmen are not new in American democracy, as is well known to those Editors who have received a phone call from President Johnson or President Kennedy, or a letter from President Truman. Television newsmen will rightly fight to maintain their independence, but they cannot be unaware that the American principle (so deeply embedded in the Constitution) that power should be distributed and subject to checks and balances, could one day be applied to the great TV networks.

In the wake of the Agnew onslaught it is reported that Congressional investigations are to be made into certain alleged malpractices of TV journalism. Did CBS finance an attempted 'invasion' of Haiti? Were demonstrators supplied with stage-prop banners for a 'protest' sequence on TV? Whatever the facts in these particular cases, television's need for action pictures does create temptations which raise important questions of editorial ethics.

While there may be nothing wrong in asking someone to walk out of his front door a second time in order to get a better picture, can the same innocence be claimed if a demonstrator is asked by a cameraman to throw a brick through the window for the benefit of the 22-inch screen? If payment is made for the exclusive right to film an event (such as the so-called 'invasion of Haiti') is that legitimate journalistic enterprise or not? Is the TV company guilty of helping to manufacture an artificial event, or can this accusation only be made if the event depends on the money paid by the TV company? If a TV documentary producer wants to film a drug party, is he guilty of 'faking' or 'staging' if he specially invites people to a party for the purpose of taking drugs and pays for their time and the use of the premises? Was it wrong, or praiseworthy, for a TV company to finance and film tunnelling escapes in Berlin?

Such questions have only to be posed to show the variety of ethical problems which may confront the conscientious TV newsman or documentary maker. In fairness it must be emphasized that the technicalities of television may require that arrangements (as to location, setting, participants) be made in advance and be paid for. Such arrangements do not necessarily amount to 'faking' or 'staging' or 'financing'. But the border-line is not easy to decide. Producers and cameramen are frequently tempted into staging, even creating, artificial events and situations for the convenience of the camera. Another questionable technique is reconstruction, either with genuine participants or actors, to depict an event at which the cameras could not be present. Surely such reconstruction should always be clearly labelled as such, and should always be carried out with scrupulous fidelity to fact. Even then the dangers remain. Where do you draw the line between dramatised documentary and documentary drama, between fictional realism and realistic fiction?

The main problem about all these border-line techniques of staging, creating, or reconstructing events is that even if they are used with the most scrupulously honest intentions, their use is bound to arouse suspicion when disclosed, and thereby to undermine public confidence in all television journalism, bringing it, unfairly, into general disrepute.

The use of dishonest techniques in documentary television is, I think, rare. But the nature of the medium does create special temptations. These must be sternly resisted, even at the expense of vivid or exclusive material.

There are conflicting theories about the effect of television violence. There are those who believe that television's continual display of *real* war and *real* violence, sandwiching that reality in between the fictional violence of gangster films and westerns, leads in time to indifference, even to a dumb acceptance of war and violence as part of the normal night's entertainment. I find such psychological speculation to be too far-fetched; I do not believe it to be true. All the evidence is that public opinion *has* been shocked and stunned by television's saturation coverage of Vietnam, and of the war in Nigeria.

Another view is that far from encouraging an aversion for or indifference to bloodshed, television has the opposite effect. That in its portrayal of real violence—war, assassinations, violent demonstrations —television inspires imitation, and spreads violence and disruption like a deadly contagion. There is much evidence of this; but one must remember that violence and disorder existed long before the television age. The casual connection between television and violence is hard to prove conclusively. Nonetheless the danger cannot be ignored, and those responsible for television should work on the assumption that television *can* incite violence and that therefore the medium should be used with restraint and responsibility.

Writing about the recent impact of television in America, Theodore H. White suggests that the advent of the half-hour national news programmes in the early 1960s created a new demand by television for dramatic pictures of action and violence, not only of the Vietnam war but of the racial conflict at home. To Mr White this was a landmark in American history as significant as the creation of the first coast-to-coast railway a hundred years ago. The growth and drawing-power of these half-hour evening news shows depended, he says, on their pictorial presentation of violence, conflict and excitement. They whetted America's appetite for sensation. Mr White, who is himself professionally involved in television, frankly admits a share of the responsibility, and he writes in *The Making of the President 1968*[1]:

'. . . one irrevocable cowardice binds all men in television—television dare not be dull. The logic is simple: if a television show is dull, then it loses its audience; if it loses its audience, it loses either sponsorship or executive protection; if it loses these the Producer goes broke or is removed. Whether television feeds on excitement, breeds excitement or provokes excitement is a matter of intricate debate. Whatever the answer is, there can be no doubt that television *spreads* excitement, and any producer, knowingly or not, recognises that the law of his survival requires that he speed the spread.'

Mr White's comments should be seen in their restricted context—the impact of American television, which operates under such ruthless pressures. But television's demand for sensation and violence is a

[1]Published by Jonathan Cape.

natural and universal characteristic of the medium; the American system has stimulated and satisfied that demand.

The lessons for other societies are clear. Television journalists must exercise their enormous responsibility with restraint and self-discipline. Under whatever system television may be financed, the dangers of seeking the maximum audience must be recognized and prevented. A system financed by advertising must be so regulated as to prevent commercial pressures from being the prevailing consideration in the minds of the programme makers. Where a publicly financed television service is in direct competition with a commercial network, the temptation to concentrate on beating them at their own game should be resisted.

CURIOSITY, YELLOW

Perhaps the most difficult question which lies upon a television editor's conscience is this: Does television by its very presence at an event help to create an explosive atmosphere of excitement and disorder? Does the presence of the camera automatically raise the temperature? Is television an incubator of violence? Here again history reminds us that men rose in bloody rebellion and violent demonstration long before the age of television. There is, however, abundant evidence that the television camera, with its power to communicate a single incident to millions who are not personally present, can act as an invitation to violence, to disorder, to revolutionary protest by dramatic physical action.

In situations of intolerable injustice is such reaction to be deplored? Perhaps not—but the question provokes counter-questions: Is not the increasing tendency of television to encourage protest by violence, rather than protest by peaceful persuasion, to invite the irrational rather than the rational response? Does not television have a built-in tendency to encourage the remedying of injustice by revolutionary action rather than by constitutional process? Again those are questions which you will answer according to individual philosophy. Some may feel it is good that television should be on the side of the 'inevitable revolution'. Others may feel there are still some problems, even in universities, which can be best solved by reasoned argument, democratic process, and peaceful change.

At this point one notices one of the confusing paradoxes of this subject. Television, which can encourage a pacifist revulsion against

war, may also be an incubator of violent revolution! An explanation of
this paradox is that the one is an effect on detached spectators, the other
is an effect on involved participants. The new revolutionary Left will
probably deny the existence of any paradox, and will say television is
merely reflecting two sides of 'objective truth'—that wars are the hid-
eous product of capitalist power politics and that revolutions are a
blessed release from bourgeois oppression.

There are many illustrations of how television does not merely
'cover' or report events, but helps to *create* events, and to transform
situations. One way in which television does this is by making people
who have hitherto accepted certain situations aware of new forces and
changing moods. Three examples may be given.

1. There is no doubt that the Negro revolution in America has been
massively accelerated by television. Not merely by spreading the idea
of violent protest, but by carrying to millions of previously apathetic
people the arguments and peaceful protest of men like Martin Luther
King. And by communicating to black Americans two fundamental
features of White America—its enviable standard of living, and its
great ideal (not always attained, but ideals nevertheless) of equal rights
and democratic opportunity. These ideals are infectious, and television
has helped to spread them with explosive consequences.

2. A second occasion was in Czechoslovakia during the brief period
of experiment in combining socialism with freedom. I was a witness
at that time to how television in Czechoslovakia had given momentum
to the freedom movement. Here was a case where TV helped create a
situation which led in turn to a major act of international policy, the
Russian invasion. Here also was a rare and memorable instance of
television being used to project and disseminate an idea. Great courage
was necessary.

3. A third example has been seen recently in a corner of the United
Kingdom. I refer to Northern Ireland. Here is a community which for
many years has been a political backwater, suffering from the deeply
entrenched prejudices of religion and communal division. The long-
standing bitterness between Catholic and Protestant made it seem as if
Northern Ireland were shut off from movements and ideas in the outside world. But then, gradually, into the remote inward-looking
communities of Ulster came a new factor: television.

And with television, came not only quiz-games and soap opera, but
startling and thought-provoking pictures of the world outside, of a

world which was changing fast. A world in which Catholics and Protestants were talking of ecumenical co-operation, a world in which the very authority of the Pope was being challenged and criticized among his own flock. A world in which people who were denied reasonable human rights on grounds of religion or race were rising up to demand them. A world in which young people, especially students, were spearheading a challenge to established authority and entrenched attitudes.

This was the world which television brought with increasing impact into the lonely cottages and the shabby back-street homes of Northern Ireland. My clear impression, supported by personal observation, is that this had a fundamental effect on Northern Ireland. It opened windows on to a broader view of the world; it helped stir a challenge to blinkered bigotry and traditional intolerance; it gave impetus to the civil rights movement, and to the policy of building bridges between the two religious communities.

Having helped to change the mood in Ulster, television was then faced with a new responsibility when serious violence exploded. Would television reporting of such violence provoke even more violence by imitation or retaliation? Would television coverage of acts of violence tend to spread that violence in a country which was largely peaceful and so distort and inflame the situation? Here, in miniature, British television had a taste of the American problem for the first time.

If anyone doubts the power of television to enlighten and to inflame let him look at the Republic of South Africa, where there is no television at all. Those who rule the land of *Apartheid* have no doubts whatever about the dangers of television to their philosophy. It is true that the introduction of television is now being planned—but with a care and caution which will ensure that South Africa is not polluted by any dangerous notions about racial equality and radical protest which television from the outside could so powerfully project.

I shall mention another aspect of television's impact on world events and opinion. Television tends to emphasize the personality of national leaders in a new way. President Kennedy was known to the world as no other American President before him. Both President Kennedy and President Johnson projected, by their own television images, an image of their country in themselves. Kennedy's personality had one effect—Johnson's had another. The impact of their contrasting styles and personalities as conveyed throughout the world by television may have had a significant effect on forming attitudes, mainly among ordinary people but also among governments, towards their country's policy.

Television may indeed have created a new kind of diplomacy: Diplomacy by Personality-projection and Leader-image. This 'tele-diplomacy' (as it has been called) can give a national leader the opportunity of talking directly to the people of another country—even one with whom his own nation may be in bitter dispute. Governments and diplomats are by-passed. The people are addressed in their own homes and can form their own impressions.

Twelve years ago I was the first British reporter to interview President Nasser after the Suez invasion. For nearly half an hour he gave his answers—directly to the British people. A front-page headline next day ran: 'Colonel Nasser Drops In'. James Cameron described the interview as follows:

'Sitting in the garden of his Cairo home, President Nasser leaned forward into British television screens. And he asked that we reunite in friendly relations. He thus did something that had never been done before in the history of international diplomacy. For the first time on record a national leader—submitting a major point of national policy—by-passed all protocol and sent his message into the homes of another state—at a time when the two were not in diplomatic relations.'

Whether that interview hastened the return to normal relations I do not know, but it happened. Similar interviews are now commonplace.

What can be done to guard against the dangers which I have mentioned, and to overcome the limitations, imposed and inherent, of television as a journalistic medium?

Because the visual headlines of television can have such a powerful effect, the utmost effort should be made to ensure that the basic TV news service is presented with integrity and responsibility. The editorial values of the daily news programmes can set the tone and standard for the whole of television's journalistic output. If the basic news service succumbs to television's tabloid temptations of sensationalism, distortion, and trivialization, if it lacks the courage and skill to tackle serious issues the courage and skill to tackle serious issues despite the limitations of time and technique, then a basic source of facts for an entire nation will be adulterated.

There were fears that this might happen when commercial television started in Britain. But it did not. The news service (Independent Television News), under the editorship of Sir Geoffrey Cox, established high standards of accuracy and responsibility. This meant that ITN's challenge to the BBC news was stimulating, and not degrading, as it might otherwise have been.

If the basic television news service goes 'yellow' then the standards of the surrounding output are liable to be lowered and corrupted. A television news service needs to be clear and lively viewing. But making cheap impact on the viewers is, in the long run, less rewarding than winning their respect for accuracy, reliability, and fairness.

In many countries, radio is a more important medium of communication than either television or the press. Though lacking the permanence of the printed word, radio broadcasting is in many ways a more satisfactory medium of information and education than television. Radio has a vast potential. The safeguards I suggest for the development of television apply equally to radio.

A good basic news service is essential, but not, by itself, enough. It must be supplemented by deeper programmes of analysis, comment, and enquiry. These may be in the form of film documentaries or studio discussion. Such programmes are essential if the visual headlines of the daily news are to be given meaning and perspective; this is particularly necessary where complex international issues are involved.

Even then television will be inadequate. Newspapers, periodicals, and books are not rendered unnecessary in the television age. On the contrary, they are more vital to a civilized and democratic society than ever. Television can shock, can stir consciences, can illuminate. But only the printed word can give a society its intellectual dynamic. Only the printed word can give full exercise to the critical faculty, and can provide an adequate instrument for the discussion and development of ideas.

It is true that technological advances may soon make possible the cheap mass production of recording and play-back equipment by which a viewer in his own home, at his own time, will be able to draw in a vast library of visual material—drama, history, academic lectures, scientific demonstration, technical instruction. Television viewing would not be confined to the ephemeral transmissions which an ordinary television service offers. But that is yet to come, and its importance lies more in education than in the communication of news and topical events to a mass audience.

Television should be run under a system which is designed to give it the maximum freedom and independence from government or commercial pressure. Needless to say, such a system is unlikely to develop in any country which is authoritarian. Nor is such a system necessarily a feature of countries which like to call themselves democratic. In de Gaulle's France, for example, television was a tool of the state.

THE VITAL PRINCIPLE

Britain has developed a very reasonable, though not perfect, system. We have two kinds of TV—public service and commercial. As a TV journalist I have worked in both.

The BBC is a public service financed by public funds—but not by direct government grant. Its income comes to the BBC from the annual licence paid by everyone who owns a television set. The BBC charter, granted periodically by Parliament, establishes it as a public (but not government-controlled) service. Though it is the Government which fixes the licence fee from which the BBC derives its income, governments do not interfere with the content of the programmes. They have been known, of course, to try (and people pick up telephones and talk to other people).

After less than fifty years' existence the BBC is regarded (abroad, at least) as one of Britain's finest achievements. Its political independence and professional standards are envied and respected as an example to broadcasters in many countries. But its independence and standards will not be upheld without constant vigilance against political pressures and the temptation to win audiences by lowering standards.

On the commercial side, television in Britain is organized in a way designed to achieve the benefits, but avoid the worst abuses, of commercial advertising. There is no direct sponsoring of programmes. Advertisers buy time—as they buy space in newspapers—and have no control over programme content. Standards ultimately depend on the determination and critical concern of the Independent Television Authority, entrusted by Parliament with the power, and the duty, to ensure 'quality' and 'balance' in programmes.

In a television service financed by advertising there is bound to be a general pressure to make programmes with maximum audience appeal, but this may also occur under a publicly financed system, especially if it is in competition with a commercial network. What safeguard is there against this process leading to a wholesale degradation of standards? There is no safeguard, except the integrity of the programme-makers and the strength of purpose in those entrusted with ultimate responsibility.

I mention these two complementary systems as examples of how a democratic society can organize and finance television in a way which enables it to be as politically independent as possible, and which, given strong leadership, can enable it to operate with reasonable fairness and responsibility. Most visitors to Britain find that our television compares favourably with that endured by most other countries. But it has many faults and the problems of television are still in their infancy.

There is no justification for complacency. There is a continual need to resist pressures from governments and commercial interests. There is a continual need to fight for standards.

The vital principle to uphold is that television is too important to be dominated either by politicians or by advertisers. That should be the aim in any mature democracy. The slogan for television's development should be independence, integrity, and diversity. Independence from political and commercial pressures. Integrity in those who make programmes. Diversity in the control and production of programmes.

There is in Britain one regrettable restriction. Television is forbidden to put its cameras into Parliament. In this we are behind certain European countries (such as Denmark and Sweden) and the United States, where Senate Committees (such as the Fulbright hearings on Vietnam) are televised with important consequences on opinion and policy.

If television is to give less trivial coverage of political issues it must be able to televise the nation's prime forum of debate. And that, in Britain, is the House of Commons.

I have long campaigned for this, not in the interests of television but in the interests of Parliament. How can Parliament expect to maintain its position as the prime forum of debate if it shuts itself off from the prime medium of mass communication?

Other essentials for the responsible use of television as a journalistic medium are these:

Television should not be completely in the hands of people whose main interest is light entertainment. Whatever system is devised should ensure that the information and journalistic side of television should be the direct responsibility of professionals concerned with the integrity of mass-communication, whose purpose is to inform, explain, and enquire. Otherwise informative television will be squeezed out by pressure to be sensational or 'entertaining' and to avoid certain awkward or unpopular subjects.

When politicians or any public figures have access to the powerful platform of television, they should be open to questioning of a critical and challenging nature. This prevents television from becoming simply a propaganda vehicle. It also offers a way in which television can deal with ideas in a serious and illuminating way. I hear the phrase 'talking head' again, but the fact is that searching political interviews have provided some of the most discussed and most controversial programmes on British television.

Probing interviews with public personalities are only one way in which television can, if it is properly run, present ideas and issues in a way which is both vivid and responsible. Film documentaries and 'live' debates are among the other methods. The important thing is that they should be presented on the assumption that the public want to know, and even if they don't, have a *right* to know.

If these and the other principles I have mentioned are adhered to, television will not simply be a new 'opium for the people'. That danger exists if television is used simply for entertainment, as an instrument of mass hypnosis to distract attention from the real world, as a tranquillizer and a trivializer. Where television is used as a medium of news and information, what I have urged may prevent it from becoming merely a projector of crude shock images—a nightly kaleidoscope of sensational happenings in the world.

One's attitude to television and how it should be used is bound to be an extension of the kind of society in which one believes. I happen to believe in a free society where governments can be changed, and grievances can be redressed, by persuasion, argument and constitutional process. I work in television in the belief that this fantastically potent medium can be used to strengthen that kind of society. I believe also that television's first duty is not to government, nor to any prevailing trend of opinion, whether among the masses or the influential few. Television's first duty is to the honest search for truth.

That is not a meaningless aspiration. Truth may be an elusive ideal. But there is the world of difference between a television service which is erected to *suppress* truth and one which is erected to *search* for it. To that end I want to see television not simply a gigantic image machine with one knob marked '*shock*' and the other marked TRANQUILLIZE. For all its limitations it can be a mighty forum of ideas—inquiring, criticizing, exposing, illuminating. Television *can* be a weapon against prejudice, injustice, and ignorance. But only if it can work in freedom, responsibility, and independence. More than 300 years ago John Milton made his historic protest against restrictions on the liberty of printing in England, and his words could well be the finest motto a television service could have today:

'*Let Truth and Falsehood Grapple; Who ever knew Truth put to the worse, in a free and open encounter?*'

PART III

The Case for Televising Parliament

The Case for Televising Parliament[1]

In February 1975 the House of Commons voted by a massive majority for a radio experiment in the broadcasting of its proceedings. This was a historic decision which future generations may see as comparable in importance to other great developments in our democratic process—the admission of reporters in the eighteenth century, the Reform Bill of 1832 and the universal franchise. But a television experiment was again rejected—though by a very few votes.

So the Case for Televising Parliament which I first argued more than fifteen years ago and published in pamphlet form in 1963 has still to be accepted. Resistance will remain strong. It is, however, an excellent thing that when television is next debated the results of the radio experiment will have shown MPs that speech extracts can be edited fairly and clearly.

Since I first argued the case for televising Parliament that case has been enormously reinforced by the dangers which have come to confront our democracy in the TV age. Television has enormous power to project unreason and violence. But that power can and should be used to project reason, and democratic discussion. If television, which is the main mass medium of news and opinion, is forbidden to project that reasoned process which is the heart of our democratic society, what sort of society will we become?

One wet and windy night this year a small group of men were huddled together underneath dripping umbrellas in Parliament Square, a few feet from Abraham Lincoln's Statue. The time was 10.15 p.m. and the date Monday, June 17th 1963. Across the Square, the House of Commons had just voted in the most critical division for many years, after the debate on the Profumo scandal.

The men who sheltered under the umbrellas were Members of Parliament and reporters. They were taking part in a BBC television report on the division, in which 27 Conservatives abstained. The MPs

[1]Originally published as a Hansard Society Pamphlet in 1963.

has rushed out from the lobbies to join the *Panorama* outside broadcast team waiting across the road in Parliament Square.

The news, the occasion, and the weather made it a dramatic broadcast. But it was a lamentably awkward and secondhand way of using television. Many people, including MPs, suddenly realized how television is hamstrung in its efforts to communicate important parliamentary proceedings to the public. A typical comment came from the TV critic of the *Daily Mail*:

'Though my own feelings have never been more than luke-warm towards the idea of televising Parliament, the Profumo debate was obviously a strong argument in favour of it . . . you felt that television's attempts to report and analyse the progress were a very feeble substitute indeed for being able to see and judge for yourself.'

There was no question of televising the debate itself, for Parliament still shuts its doors against the television cameras as firmly as it shut them against newspaper reporters in bygone days.

There was not even the possibility of getting rooms inside the Parliament buildings as studio centres for the service which the TV networks were seeking to provide throughout the debate. So the BBC operated outside in the Square, and Independent Television News set up a makeshift studio in a nearby pub.

Such were the best arrangements which could be made for television coverage of this crucial parliamentary event. No incident has done more to strengthen the case for televising Parliament.

Until recently the thought of TV cameras in the House of Commons was repugnant to all except a very few. But with television firmly established as part of the press and of public life, the idea has steadily gained favour both inside Parliament and out. It has become increasingly evident that Parliament, *in its own interest*, should not continue to shut itself off from the television cameras.

Six years ago, after suffering the frustrations of a parliamentary reporter trying to describe six-hour debates in two-minute verbal reports on TV, I began asking leading parliamentarians about televising the House. 'Over my dead body' was the most frequent reply, but some at least were open-minded. Even so, no one took it very seriously.

When the Canadians televised the State Opening of their Parliament by the Queen, recordings of this ceremony were seen in Britain. The

BBC promptly applied for permission to televise our own State Opening at Westminster. In the following year, 1958, after many doubts and misgivings, Government and Opposition eventually agreed that this could be done. The television coverage was hailed as brilliant and the Constitution survived.

Television had entered Parliament for the first time, though the Government declared that there was no intention of allowing cameras into the ordinary business of Parliament. The broadcast made constitutional history. Television enabled all the people to witness an ancient parliamentary ritual previously seen only by a privileged few. As a television spectacle it was second only in splendour to the Coronation. But to me, working as a commentator for this ceremony, it did not seem right that television should be admitted only to show the pageantry and the symbolism, while being excluded from the working life of Parliament.

At first only a very small minority of MPs shared this opinion. But gradually the growth of the television audience and the problems of political broadcasting made more and more MPs revise their views. It was not until Aneurin Bevan sprang a surprise on everybody by advocating the televising of Parliament, that the Government was forced to think about it seriously for the first time. Mr Bevan was speaking in the debate on the Address in 1959:

'At the beginning of this Parliament I am going to suggest that a serious investigation takes place into the technical possibilities of televising Parliamentary proceedings.'
Mr Cyril Osborne (Louth): 'Oh, no, Nye.'
Mr Bevan: 'I know that Members shake their heads, but why should they be so shy? . . . All I am suggesting is that in these days when all the apparatus of mass suggestion are against democratic education, we should seriously consider re-establishing intelligent communication between the House of Commons and the Electorate as a whole. That, surely, is a democratic process.'

In one or two private arguments Mr Bevan had tackled me vigorously about the problems of televising Parliament, but he had quickly grasped the essential point that Parliament should not be shut off from the power of television. I was less surprised than others when he made his suggestion from the despatch box. What particularly disturbed him was the system under which politicians were granted access to television's powerful platform. This was one of the main arguments he gave for televising Parliament:

'Recently, and not only recently but for many years now, there has grown up what I consider a most humiliating state of affairs in which Members of the House are picked out to take part in television broadcasts at the *ipse dixit* of the bureaucracy at Broadcasting House. In fact there has been nothing more humiliating than to see Members of Parliament in responsible positions selected by unrepresentative persons to have an opportunity of appearing on the radio or television. . . . Also, what is almost worse, political alternatives are not placed before the people in a realistic fashion because of the selection of speakers that takes place. I have complained about this on many occasions.'

Unfortunately Mr Bevan followed up his powerful argument with a proposal that made even the most ardent advocate of televising Parliament blanch:

'There ought to be a special channel that they can turn on and listen to us at any time. I am not arguing that we should have only special debates televised, but that there should be a special channel for the House of Commons itself. . . .'

Mr Bevan's case for televising Parliament had been impressive, but his idea of a complete and continuous transmission was widely ridiculed. It distracted attention from the strength of his main argument. No other way of televising Parliament was discussed on that occasion.

It seemed to me that an alternative method was much more likely to gain acceptance—a late-evening *Television Hansard*, which would be an *edited* recording of the day's proceedings, varying in length according to what had happened. A TV *Hansard* on these lines, I felt, would avoid all the main objections to Mr Bevan's proposal. This case was argued for the first time in a letter I wrote to *The Times* on November 11th 1959:

'Sir,—Mr Bevan's suggestion that Parliament should be continuously televised on a special channel has met with much criticism. As a television reporter who has done his best to describe parliamentary debates in the space of two or three minutes, I have long been in favour of televising Parliament. But I suggest that Mr Bevan's proposal is not the way to do it.

'What is needed is a late-evening *Television Hansard*, which would be an edited recording of the day's proceedings. It would vary in length according to what had happened.

'This *Television Hansard* could be run by a Parliamentary Television Unit, financed out of public funds, operating from Westminster. This unit would have the duty of presenting a fair selection of extracts from the proceedings. Its authority to operate would be periodically reviewed by Parliament.

'A *Television Hansard* on these lines would avoid the main objections to Mr Bevan's proposal:

'1. It would not monopolize a special channel.

'2. It would enable Question Time and important statements made in the afternoon to be seen in the evening by a much bigger audience.

'3. There would be no problem as to which MPs are called at peak viewing hours. All would have a reasonable chance of inclusion in a late-evening edited report.

'4. Tedious procedural matters could be omitted. Mr Gaitskell need not fear that "hours of infinite boredom" would be inflicted on the public.

'May I deal with three objections which are bound to be raised against my proposal?

'1. Is it technically possible? I would think it is, but this is a matter for a full expert inquiry which would pay special attention to the problem of televising without any annoyance to Members or interference with normal procedure.

'2. Is it possible to present an edited report of Parliament, with selected extracts of speeches, in such a way as to give general satisfaction? This might be difficult, but I do not see why it should be more difficult than the job of compiling *Today in Parliament* which the BBC does every night on the radio.

'3. Would there not be a danger of MPs talking to the cameras instead of to each other? When Mr Herbert Morrison raised this point (on February 3rd last) the Prime Minister commented that this was exactly the argument which was presented against the publication of *Hansard*.

'There is an important constitutional argument for televising Parliament which should be added to those cited by Mr Bevan. The television balance is now tilted heavily in favour of the Government. This is due to the continual appearances of Ministers, whose doings inevitably make frequent news items for television. The only way to redress this balance is to televise Parliament. Not only would the viewer see more regular statements of anti-Government views, but Ministers would be spared many of the television appearances they are now expected to make in addition to their parliamentary statements.

'The case for an inquiry into the possibility of a *Television Hansard* is overwhelming. Parliament should not be as blind and stubborn towards television as it was in its unhappy struggle with the press.

'Yours faithfully
Robin Day'

This idea of an edited version has now become generally accepted as the method which would have to be used if Parliament is ever televised on a public channel.

As a result of Mr Bevan's request for a technical investigation into the possibilities of televising Parliament, the Government asked the BBC to make a report. This was not published. Nor were any experiments conducted.

Since 1960 the subject has kept cropping up at Question Time, and in March 1963 when the House debated Mr Charles Pannell's motion on parliamentary reform, the question of televising the House had become sufficiently important for front-bench speakers on both sides to deal with it at some length. The most conservative view came from the Labour Chief Whip, Mr Herbert Bowden. He attacked the whole idea as 'frightening', and said:

'I do not like the idea ... I do not want Parliament to become an alternative to *That Was The Week That Was*, or *Steptoe & Son* or *Coronation Street*.'

Mr Bowden was giving his personal view—which is not shared by all his front-bench colleagues. Mr James Callaghan, for instance, is strongly in favour of televising Parliament. (Speech reported in *The Times*, July 9th 1962.)

The Liberal leader, Mr Jo Grimond, announced his conversion in the same debate:

'I used to be against the idea of televising the House of Commons but it is an essential function of the House to raise issues and get them across to the public. I do not want the House televised direct in session, but I want a programme like *Today in Parliament* put on at night because I think this is a great function.'

The most significant contribution came from Mr Iain Macleod. He too spoke personally, but with all the weight of his position as Leader of the House of Commons. Mr Macleod's remarks came as a complete break with orthodox parliamentary opinion about television. Emphasizing that it was a matter for the House to decide, he recalled the groundless anxieties about televising the Coronation and the Party Conferences. Referring to Mr Bowden's hostility to televising Parliament, Mr Macleod declared:

'Frankly, I disagree with him. . . . I myself think there is a great deal to be said for it. I agree with the leader of the Liberal Party.'

He added that he could see a considerable case for an edited version, television's *Today in Parliament*.

Since that debate, an interesting variant of the plan for an edited version has been persuasively canvassed by a member of the Cabinet, Mr William Deedes, Minister without Portfolio. The argument runs as follows. In order to present a late-night edited version to the public on TV, the cameras would have to be running continuously and expensively all day. Mr Deedes wants to make fuller use of this continuous camera coverage by having it 'piped live' on closed circuit to certain institutions such as universities, newspaper offices, clubs, etc. These organizations would pay a special subscription for this service. Mr Deedes points to two advantages of this scheme. First, the educational value to students and others. Second, the financial contribution which these special subscriptions could make towards the very high cost of televising Parliament.

This would certainly be a very useful arrangement if enough special subscribers are interested, but my own view is that it should not be regarded as a substitute for an evening edited version, on a public channel for the entire TV audience, at a time when ordinary people who work during the day could tune in if they wish.

Despite the weight of Mr Macleod's support, and the growing interest among other parliamentarians, the idea of televising Parliament is still repugnant to many MPs. Some, while not hostile, are doubtful about the proposal to televise proceedings in edited form. Others are worried about the possible inconvenience and distraction (cameras, lights, etc.) and about television's effect on the atmosphere of debate. From conversations with MPs who are against the whole idea it is clear that many of the arguments have not been clearly put to them. This is not surprising. The question has never been fully debated in the House, nor investigated by a Select Committee.

The purpose of this pamphlet is therefore to set out the case for televising parliamentary proceedings in edited form and to urge that a Select Committee of the House enquire into all aspects of the question —constitutional, technical and financial.

WHY TELEVISE PARLIAMENT?

There are many compelling reasons why the televising of Parliament would be immensely beneficial to the public, to broadcasting, to democracy and to Parliament itself.

1. Authentic political debate could be seen on the TV screen.
The viewer would see debates between those who have the political responsibility. Parliament may all too often be a disappointing forum, but it is at least preferable to staged studio discussions between hack controversialists brought in from Westminster or Fleet Street. Television discussions about politics may stimulate and entertain, but they are not the real thing. One difficulty with these discussions is that they can be killed by a Minister's refusal to take part. The programme may have to be cancelled. This means that the rule of 'balance' can be used as an instrument of censorship. At best, the discussion proceeds with a loyal backbencher put up as the Minister's understudy. He may perform well, but he cannot speak with the same authority as the man responsible, the Minister. The discussion is virtually crippled.

A *Television Hansard* would ensure that any issue discussed by the Commons is seen by the viewer in its parliamentary setting. Instead of seeing Cabinet Ministers (when they consent) interrogated only by professional TV interviewers, the public would see them regularly confronted by those to whom they are constitutionally responsible. Television interviewing, if it is vigorous and incisive, can be a useful form of journalism. It is no substitute for parliamentary questioning or debate.

2. Parliament would no longer be shut off from the most powerful medium of mass communication.

The press can report Parliament as fully as it wishes. Television, denied direct coverage, cannot do more than present the briefest verbal accounts, or interviews from makeshift studios outside the House. No television technique has yet been found (even by ITN's enterprising *Dateline Westminster*) which adequately conveys the arguments, let alone the atmosphere, of a parliamentary debate. How can Parliament's prestige be maintained if the work of its members goes largely unseen by the modern mass audience? By permitting the entry of television, Parliament would ensure that this potent magnifier of reputations is not monopolized by quiz panellists, announcers, commentators, university dons, and politicians who have failed to be elected.

3. A Television Hansard *would solve a crucial problem of British broadcasting: the mistrust and alarm which the increasingly critical independence of TV journalism has aroused in both big political parties.*

This is a point which may not be generally appreciated. Over the last few years the growth of journalistic freedom in broadcasting, especially in television, has been tremendous. The duty of impartiality has been interpreted in a more robust and independent spirit. The inevitable, but not intended, result has been that the effect of some programmes may have appeared biased against the Government. The longer the Government has been in power the more noticeable and more natural has this tendency become. This may suit the Opposition at the present time, but they are fully aware that this critical independence, steadily achieved in the formative years of mass television, will not suddenly die away if a Labour Government comes to power. I have heard it argued—and this is the crux of the matter—that a Labour Government might feel itself to be in an intolerable situation if, in addition to a 'predominantly anti-Labour press', the 'supposedly impartial' TV networks maintain a critical independence whose effect might appear anti-Government.

Such a situation might, it is hinted, lead to Government pressure, and attempts to curb the hard-won independence of TV journalism. Alternatively, on the more generous assumption that a Labour Government would resist any temptation to suppress or interfere with programmes, the mere prospect of such pressure might cause the TV authorities to order more caution and restraint in topical programmes.

Both these possibilities hold the most serious implications for the future of British television. Both would mean putting the clock back ten years or more. But if Parliament were televised the situation would be transformed. Any temptation to curb the vigorous impartiality of TV journalism would be removed. For whatever the effect of ordinary TV programmes, a *Television Hansard* would ensure that the Government's case would be regularly put before the public, just as clearly and as effectively as it may be put before Parliament. What could be fairer?

Equally, televising Parliament would dispel the misgivings of the many Conservatives who may not be convinced that TV journalism would, in fact, continue to be as critical under a Labour Government. For if Parliament were televised the Opposition's case would be presented on the screen as frequently and as fully as the Government's.

This reasoning is based on the conviction that a *Television Hansard*, with its potentially vast audience for debates on big issues, would develop into the most influential forum of public affairs on television. If I am right in this belief, other programmes featuring political discussions and interviews would cease to possess the importance with which they are now credited. In this way the uneasiness felt in both big parties about television's critical spirit would be allayed if Parliament were televised.

4. *Whichever party happens to be in power, the televising of Parliament would bring much benefit to both sides.*
Ministers would benefit, not only from the regular platform of a *Television Hansard* but by being burdened with fewer TV appearances in addition to their parliamentary duties. I once saw the Prime Minister give three airport interviews at seven-thirty in the morning after an all-night flight from America. A *Television Hansard* could have transmitted the more important statement which he made to the House shortly afterwards. A Cabinet Minister who makes an important statement in the House sometimes repeats it more than once for TV.

Otherwise he does not personally explain it to the viewing public at all. Either procedure is unsatisfactory. A *Television Hansard* would avoid both.

Opposition leaders would benefit because a regular *Television Hansard* would enable their views on specific topics to be seen in daily juxtaposition to those of Ministers. At present a Government has a natural advantage in TV news programmes, because Ministers are always making news with decisions and announcements. An Opposition also makes news in various ways, but its comments on an issue may not be so newsworthy as a Ministerial pronouncement on the same subject.

5. *Other vexed and artificial problems of political broadcasting would be largely swept away:*

(a) Political 'balance' would no longer be a crucial problem in topical programmes. If MPs have a fair and regular chance of being seen in a *Television Hansard*, the illusory search for 'balance' would cease to cause daily headaches at Lime Grove, Television House, or at party headquarters. A simple clash between official party spokesmen is easy to arrange but it may not reflect the real division of opinion. As Sir William Haley described his experience as Director-General of the BBC: '. . . it was child's play to keep the balance *between* the parties; it was a very difficult thing to keep the balance *within* the parties.'

(b) 'Ministerial' broadcasts would rarely be needed and problems arising from them would no longer be crucial. These are the so-called 'non-political' broadcasts by Ministers on matters of national importance. The Opposition may seek to reply if they consider a Ministerial broadcast is controversial, as Mr Gaitskell did after Sir Anthony Eden's Suez broadcast. The BBC has to decide whether such a broadcast is controversial or not. A similar situation may arise when the Prime Minister is 'invited' to broadcast on a major national issue.[1] Why should such invidious decisions, however fair-mindedly they are made, rest with the broadcasting authorities? A *Television Hansard* would enable Ministerial broadcasts of national importance to be made from the proper place—the Government despatch box, and answered from the proper place—the Oppposition despatch box.

(c) Party political broadcasts could be abolished. These broadcasts,

[1] In such situations the Opposition now has an unconditional right of reply. See BBC Handbook 1975, p. 216.

widely acknowledged as being poor politics and worse television, are transmitted at peak hours on both channels at the same time. They leave the wretched viewer, who may be already converted, or beyond conversion, no alternative. A *Television Hansard* would enable the public to see their political leaders in the nation's prime forum of debate—Parliament.

6. *The system by which MPs have opportunities to appear on television would be put on a much fairer basis.*
There are two ways in which this would happen:

(a) Minority opinion, as voiced in parliamentary debate, would get a fairer share on the screen This applies not only to the Liberals, but also to rebel or dissenting groups within the big parties. Though unorthodox views are now broadcast more often than in the past, there still exists the ever-ready pressure of the Whips and party machines to keep 'representative' (i.e. official) opinion to the fore when MPs appear in TV discussions. There is, moreover, that peak-hour perquisite of party orthodoxy, the TV space allocated on both channels for 'party political broadcasts'.

The individual heretic, the lone parliamentary dissenter, has traditionally been able to catch the Speaker's eye. With the cameras in the House he would catch the public eye on television more often than he is able to at present. A *Television Hansard* would ensure that a Churchill of the future would not be restricted from broadcasting his warnings about the Gathering Storm.

(b) MPs would not be so dependent for their access to TV's platform on the arbitrary choice of TV executives who produce topical programmes. This was one of Mr Bevan's main arguments, deploring 'the humiliating state of affairs' in which BBC or ITV officials decide which of the people's representatives shall appear in TV programmes. With Parliament regularly on television the question of which MPs are invited to appear in ordinary topical programmes would become much less important. Choice (of speech extracts) would have to be exercised in editing a *Television Hansard*, but quite different considerations would then apply—see page 132.

7. *Individual injustices which are aired in Parliament and in the press could be aired on the television screen.*
Television is virtually impotent in this sphere. It is television's gravest

weakness. At present there can be brief verbal accounts of parliamentary protests, but rarely can TV cover the issues adequately. Unlike the press, it can rarely make investigations into individual cases or expose injustices involving legal charges or official misdemeanours. This is partly due to the impartiality rule which may prevent any discussion if one side refuses to appear. It is also due to the lack of space to make detailed investigations into individual cases. There is the further danger of libel, a matter on which the TV authorities are even more cautious than the press. In television, libel risks are very seldom taken and actions are rarely fought. A *Television Hansard* would be free to report anything raised in Parliament. It would provide an entirely new platform for the exposure of justice and incompetence.

8. Television would stimulate the House of Commons to modernize its procedure and improve the standard of debate.
Overhaul of the parliamentary machine is being demanded on all sides. A group of Conservative MPs has warned that our system of parliamentary government must 'change or decay'. Is it not reasonable to expect that if the way Parliament works is exposed by television to a much wider public, the result would be to encourage change rather than decay? MPs are not unresponsive to public opinion, and perhaps one reason why Parliament has been slow to reform itself is that few members of the electorate are aware of what is wrong. Hence there is no pressure of public opinion about parliamentary reform.

It is argued that television would encourage exhibitionism and stunts. I believe that the very opposite would happen. The knowledge that their activities were being seen in the homes of the electorate would make MPs think twice about indulging in the more vulgar habits, such as booing and cheap interruptions. Consider the known effects of the television camera. How often do we see on TV the same exhuberant crudity and extremism that is seen at political meetings, or even sometimes in Parliament? (Not often enough, to my way of thinking). Contrary to a curious misconception, the presence of the television camera has the remarkable effect of making public figures behave—and argue—more reasonably. They know that this gives a much better impression on the small screen in the quiet family circle. Television's intimacy encourages the arts of persuasion and argument. Indeed television is in danger of making controversy too calm, too civilized, too moderate. Lord Hailsham's celebrated TV interview about the Profumo scandal was an exception to prove the rule. It created a sensation and provoked strong reactions of all kinds because it was so heated and impassioned, and in complete contrast to the usual political utterance on TV.

The fear that television would destroy the traditional House of Commons atmosphere was the theme of Mr Herbert Bowden's argument when he spoke in the debate on March 15th 1963:

'Through you, Mr Speaker, we address each other in debate. We are not speaking to the country or to the world outside. It is true that reports of our debates appear in *Hansard*. But the very intimacy of our debates would be lost if the atmosphere was not as it is. . . . I am very much afraid that once the television cameras swung into action the whole atmosphere of this Chamber would change. . . .

'I have noticed that this House has its moods. It has its hilarious moods, its serious moods, and very often when an important statement is imminent we are often apprehensive and giggle and behave rather like schoolgirls. I think that is right. It is right that Members of Parliament should react in that way. If an important statement is expected, the apprehensions about what its effects may be on the country have their effects upon us. A great deal of that would be lost if it were felt that the television cameras were trained on us. Television would add nothing to our privileges or to our dignity.'

What substance is there in this argument? Whether all MPs would agree that a tendency to 'giggle like schoolgirls' is one of Parliament's precious traditions, I am not sure. Certainly no one who respects Parliament would wish to destroy the uniquely intimate atmosphere of debate. There is no evidence that television would have this effect. On the contrary, television, with its close-up pictures seen by viewers seated in twos and threes in their homes, is a medium perfectly suited to the best traditions of parliamentary behaviour. Members who sought to 'hog' the cameras by spurious points of order, or by means of 'stunt' adjournments and other procedural gimmicks, would soon incur the contempt of the public and the hostility of their fellow Members.

Then there is the fear that Members would 'play to the gallery'. Mr Macmillan gave the best answer to this point when Mr Herbert Morrison (as he then was) referred to the danger of MPs talking to the cameras, and said that debates should not be on the basis of what the public outside would like. Mr Macmillan expressed sympathy with that view but added:

'I am bound to say, if I give my personal opinion, that that was exactly the argument which was presented against the publication of *Hansard*.'

9. *There would be a new and powerful platform to counteract the mono-polistic tendencies of Fleet Street.*
At a time when famous organs of newspaper opinion have been shut down or threatened with extinction, the televising of Parliament would be one of the most effective ways in which television could, as it must, be built into an alternative platform of democratic expression.

10. *Television offers a measureless opportunity for rekindling interest in Parliament.*
The interest might well prove to be critical, but would that be un-healthy? The great need is to re-establish, as Aneurin Bevan said, 'in-telligent communication between the House of Commons and the electorate as a whole'. Nine out of ten people in Britain can now watch television in their own homes. A *Television Hansard* would give a vast new section of the public a fair idea of what Parliament is really about. Lord Hinchingbrooke, MP (as he then was) summed up the argument thus:

'Parliament must work with the tools of the age or it will sculpt no monuments for the future. If there is disillusionment with the parlia-mentary process it is because our difficulties are not shared with, and understood by, our constituents. Let the cameras reveal the facts.'

THE EDITING PROBLEM

There now appears to be general agreement that if Parliament is to be televised at all, it must be done in edited form. The main arguments for this method have already been stated.

Complete live transmission might be appropriate on special occasions, such as Budget Day, but otherwise there would be an edited report of the day's proceedings lasting from half an hour upwards and varying in length according to what had happened. It would begin fairly late at night, at, say, 10.30 p.m.

While it is agreed that continuous live transmission every day would be wholly impracticable, there is considerable doubt about how a late-night report would be edited. This is what seems to worry MPs. Who do the editing and on what principles?

When Mr Macmillan was asked about this he observed that editing would raise 'delicate problems'. This is so. The editing of *all* political news raises 'delicate problems', particularly in television news which, unlike the press, must be politically impartial. There are TV executives and commentators whose professional speciality is in handling such problems, and who would be well qualified to work on a *Television Hansard*.

Will not the process of selection place too great a power in the hands of those responsible for editing? Here it should be explained that the choice of extracts from a parliamentary debate is a very different matter from the choice of MPs invited to appear in, say, a *Panorama* or *Gallery* discussion. A topical programme like *Panorama* is initiated, devised and 'cast' by TV producers. A subject is chosen, the treatment decided and speakers are invited accordingly. Inevitably there are many MPs who are rarely, if ever, asked to appear, because the producer's choice will understandably be influenced by consideration of experience, authority or television expertise. The producer's choice may also be affected by party demands for an acceptable spokesman.

That is what happens on ordinary TV programmes, but (the distinction is crucial) a televised report of Parliament would not be a producer's creation. It would be a report of a public event. Selection of extracts from parliamentary speeches would be a matter of editorial news judgment. The selection would be openly made from a known list of speakers. Similar judgment is regularly exercised in selecting extracts to be read on radio's *Today in Parliament*, in editing TV reports of Party Conferences, and in TV coverage of election news. In all such programmes it has been found possible to handle the 'delicate problems' fairly. A further point is that a *Television Hansard* would be seen *daily*, so that if complete satisfaction could not be given to everybody on a single evening, this would be achieved over a period of time.

Who would be entrusted with producing the *Television Hansard*? This would be for the House to decide in consultation with the TV authorities. Presumably the responsibility would be offered to the BBC,

Panorama interview with Senator John F. Kennedy, Washington 1960

The Kennedy-Nixon campaign, Illinois 1960

ITN interview with Vice-President Nixon, 1958

BBC interview with Harold Wilson

or perhaps to a specially created Parliamentary Television Unit which would include personnel from both BBC and ITV. There can be little doubt that the BBC would be keenly interested in televising Parliament as a feature of its forthcoming second service, judging from the comment by Mr Kenneth Adam, Director of BBC Television:

'If cameras are admitted to the Palace of Westminster, then BBC 2 might well be the place for an extended version of *Today in Parliament*.'[1]

I do not wish to belittle the difficulties of presenting a nightly edited version. It would be a tremendous challenge, editorially and technically, even to those most experienced in political reporting on television. But with experiment and practice there is no reason why the problems should not be satisfactorily solved.

The process of editing would solve one difficulty about the TV coverage of Question Time. Mr Macmillan raised the point during an exchange on February 14th 1963:

'. . . I am not an expert, but I should have thought that it would be rather difficult to make Question Time very good from a broadcasting point of view unless the public were given an Order Paper, otherwise the proceedings would be difficult to follow.'

This would be so if Question Time were televised 'live', owing to the procedure of questions being called by number without the question on the order paper being read out. In an edited version, however, the solution would be easy. The reporter presenting the programme would insert a linking phrase (e.g. 'Mr Patrick Wall asked Mr Butler for a statement on his talks with the Prime Minister of Southern Rhodesia.). Supplementaries would be seen being put by the questioner.

This technique would enable exchanges to be selected, and questions to be followed clearly by the viewer. In introducing extracts from speeches, a similar method would be used, with the 'link' leading in to the extract (e.g. 'Mr Gordon Walker welcomed the Bill but said the Opposition would move two important Amendments').

It may be argued that some MPs speak in such a long-winded fashion that it would be hard to select short extracts which fairly represented their case. This would not always be too difficult, but in any case it is

[1]Address in Leeds University, November 1962.

6—DBD · ·

likely that television would have the wholly desirable effect of making parliamentary speeches a good deal more succinct than they are now. No doubt this will be attacked as changing the character of Parliament. Would this be so terrible? Parliament is ancient, but it has not yet fossilized. The style and length of speeches are quite different now from what they were fifty years ago. A little more crispness and clarity would not do Parliament any harm. The number of frustrated MPs who go home with undelivered speeches in their pockets would be fewer.

THE TECHNICAL PROBLEM

Perhaps the most serious anxiety felt by many MPs concerns the technical paraphernalia. Mr Charles Curran asked the Leader of the House on March 15th 1963:

'On this question of the possibility of televising our proceedings, has my right hon. Friend taken into account the difficulties that would be involved, for example, all the apparatus, gear and mechanisms which would have to be brought into the Chamber. Would that make any difference to the conducting of our Business?'

Mr Macleod replied:

'I am certain these arguments are formidable, but that they are also not insuperable.'

Mr Macmillan took the same line in answers on March 1st 1960. Basing his replies on the BBC's unpublished report, Mr Macmillan summed up technical requirements as 'a rather stronger light' and 'cameras in various parts of the galleries'. Mr Macmillan described these requirements as 'no more than rather inconvenient'.

The thought of only limited inconvenience may be extremely distasteful to many MPs. It should therefore be pointed out that Mr Macmillan's remarks were based on a preliminary survey made more than three years ago, without experiments having been made to overcome any alleged 'inconvenience'. An accurate assessment by the technical experts (of whom I am not one) can only be made after full experiment, taking into account the latest advances in electronic cameras and recording processes. If there are serious obstacles, these can only be overcome if the House of Commons indicates its positive interest in being televised by saying 'We want it. Can you do it?' This is the only way. No one would want to dislocate the procedure of Parliament by the presence of obtrusive camera equipment and the discomfort of hot arc-lamps. There has been no indication that such dislocation would result. What minor inconvenience there might be could be overcome only if experiments are permitted.

MPs would not need to be guinea-pigs when experiments are conducted. When the adjustable air-temperature system for the rebuilt House had to be tested under realistic conditions, troops from the Brigade of Guards were paraded in the Chamber as stand-ins. This admirable body of men may be less suited to perform as debaters in the parliamentary manner. There would be no difficulty in arranging for university students to take the part of MPs in mock debates during the recess. The recess would give technicians time to consider lighting adjustments, the position of cameras, and whether any minor structural alterations would be necessary in order to hide the cameras. A small Committee of the House could attend to sample the conditions, to ensure that Honourable and Right Honourable members would not be dazzled, roasted, tripped up by cables, or hit on the head by a zoom lens when they jumped up to catch the Speaker's eye. If these fears were cleared away, Parliament could then permit closed-circuit coverage of real debates, so that Members could see how the *Television Hansard* would be edited and presented to the public.

A Select Committee, therefore, should not only enquire into the constitutional and editorial aspects of televising Parliament, but at the same time should authorize full-scale technical experiments, the results of which would play a crucial part in determining the Committee's recommendations.

WHO WOULD WATCH?

How large an audience for a *Television Hansard* would there be? For big occasions, like Budget Day, or debates on issues arousing intense public interest, the audience would be vast. The BBC's special report transmitted from Parliament Square after the Profumo debate was seen by about 8 million people. This was at 10.15 p.m. The audience would have been even higher during the winter months. A slightly different example, but one illustrating the audience which can be attracted by a late-evening programme on a major political issue was to be seen in the BBC Special on the Beeching Plan (time: 10 p.m.) for which the estimated audience was 10.8 million.

Apart from such exceptional occasions it is fair to assume that for a light-night parliamentary report there would normally be a minority audience. But it should be remembered how large a 'minority' audience can be. It is relevant to note the BBC audience figures for serious political programmes late at night. The average audience for *Gallery* has been about 2½ million, and recently even larger. Party Conference reports (at 10.45 p.m.) have had audiences of similar size. When *Gallery* has presented a 'By-election special' the audience has been as high as nearly 4 million. Even when the programme continued after midnight to await the results, the BBC audience was estimated at 700,000, not to mention those watching ITV's simultaneous coverage.

These figures give some idea of the 'minority' which might, on average, watch a *Television Hansard*. Two or three million may not seem very large, but it is a very much larger number of people than those who read the parliamentary reports in papers like *The Times*, the *Guardian*, or the *Daily Telegraph*. Even if fewer than a million watched at any one time, there would be a vast number of people who might watch occasionally and would thus get some sight and understanding of what parliament does. Every day there would be something worth televising—parts of Question Time, or a Minister's statement followed by Opposition protests. The debate which follows may not always be of sensational interest, but it is bound to concern the rights or interests of somebody somewhere. Parliament would not be televised as mass entertainment but as a public service.

PARLIAMENT, PRESS AND TV

The case for a *Television Hansard* is inspired by respect for the institution of Parliament. For how can Parliament maintain its rightful importance as the nation's prime forum of debate, if it shuts itself off from the nation's prime medium of mass communication?

There are those who profess a cynical contempt for Parliament.

The House of Commons is an easy target for the attacks of sophisticated writers, who appear to confuse an assignment in the press gallery with the job of a dramatic critic. Parliament is not a show staged for the benefit of journalists. Its proceedings must often be pedestrian and tedious, but the most pedestrian debate matters to someone, and amid the long hours of tedium there are clashes of principle and moments of drama. Television would let Parliament be seen for what it is: most of the time a workshop, and some of the time a theatre.

I am not primarily concerned with the interests of television, except insofar as it is prevented from serving the democratic process more efficiently than at present. Television is not an end in itself. It is simply a means of communication and expression. The admission of the TV camera would be in Parliament's own interest.

Parliament, however, has not always been able to see where its true interests lie. Two hundred years ago Parliament was not prepared to admit that the public who had elected it had a right to know what it was doing. Yet it is impossible to conceive how modern parliamentary government could have developed without press reporting. The eighteenth-century struggles between Parliament and the press have their unmistakeable echoes in the present-day argument about televising Parliament. It was a very long time before Parliament admitted reporters or agreed to the publication of the debates. And not until the early nineteenth century was Mr T. C. Hansard providing the regular series of reports which eventually became the official record. In 1738 the House of Commons, alarmed by the 'great presumption' of journalists in reporting its proceedings, declared it 'a high indignity and notorious breach of privilege to print accounts of debates'. The main argument was the danger of misrepresentation. This fear has its equivalent today in the warnings about unfair editing of a *Television Hansard*. Another of the old arguments has an even more familiar ring in the TV age. It was urged that press reports should be forbidden because they would tend to make MPs accountable for what they said inside the House to people outside it!

Fortunately for Parliament and the country, this notion of democracy did not prevail for long. In 1771 Parliament was openly defied. Those who were consequently committed to the Tower of London became popular heroes. Their release was the occasion of a great demonstration. The House of Commons gave way and made no further attempt to enforce its order. But the reporting of Parliament is still, technically, a breach of privilege. And the ban still applies to radio and television which have firmly established themselves as part of the press. Since it is only by Parliament's authority that the broadcasting services operate at all, one can hardly expect any challenges in eighteenth-century style from the camera or microphone—even if the equipment was small enough to be smuggled in without anyone noticing.

It is to be hoped that Parliament will not be so slow and stubborn about television as it was about the press. In the seventeenth century, 'news-letters'—precursors of modern newspapers—were circulating notes on the secret happenings in Parliament. It was more than a hundred years before Parliament granted reporters a bench in their own right. How long will it be before television takes its inevitable and rightful place in the Press Gallery? It cannot be long now. The case for televising Parliament is overwhelming. Future generations, accustomed to seeing Parliament on their television screens, will wonder what all the fuss was about.

That was how I set out the arguments in the Hansard Society Pamphlet which was sent in 1963 to every Member of Parliament. By the end of the decade the case had won considerable acceptance, but the cameras were still excluded. Although new and even stronger arguments were beginning to become apparent, the 'Keep television out' campaigners had become more determined than ever. They were able to seize on some regrettable examples of unfairness or trivialization in television programmes to reinforce their implacable opposition to admitting the cameras, even for an experiment. In November 1969 I wrote the following article in The Times *to bring the story and arguments up to date.*

On November 13, 1959, *The Times* published a letter in which I put forward the idea of televising Parliament by means of edited late-night reports. The letter concluded: 'Parliament should not be as blind and stubborn towards television as it was in its unhappy struggle with the press.'

The ten years which have passed since then provide a pathetic case-history for students of our national diseases—chronic short-sightedness and incurable resistance to innovation.

At first the reaction to the idea was almost universally hostile. From most members of Parliament the short answer to the idea of televising their proceedings in any way was: 'Over my dead body.' Alone among prominent parliamentarians, Mr Aneurin Bevan, with characteristic boldness of vision, had grasped the essential point that Parliament should not be cut off from the new power of television. But his proposal for a special channel for continuous 'live' parliamentary broadcasts was open to many obvious objections. The idea of using recorded extracts for edited reports (especially in a television version of radio's long-established *Today in Parliament*) seemed to me much more practical and acceptable. The same conclusion was reached unanimously, seven years later, by an all-party Commons committee.

This reflected a slow but significant shift which had been taking place in parliamentary opinion. The 1964 and 1966 elections had brought in a younger generation of MPs. And one by one, with many expressions of caution and suspicion, leading parliamentarians had pronounced themselves in favour of admitting the cameras.

In 1965 the Commons Select Committee on Publications started an inquiry on their own initiative. This forced attention to the importance of the issue, and a select committee on the specific question of broadcasting proceedings was set up by the House.

After hearing all the evidence about technical problems and all the arguments for and against television, this committee came to the conclusion that the best way of regularly televising Parliament would be by edited extracts. The suggestion was that continuous camera coverage of the House could be available for the television networks to record, edit, and broadcast, in various ways: in daily and weekly reports, news bulletins, topical magazines, documentaries, regional programmes, and historical or educational programmes. The committee's main recommendation was that the Commons should permit a closed-circuit experiment

It appeared that progress was being made, inch by inch. The speed of advance into the twentieth century seemed positively headlong when in November 1966, the Government proposed to the Commons that a closed-circuit experiment should be conducted on the lines recommended by the select committee.

But the idea of an experiment was just too revolutionary for the House of Commons. By a majority of one, on a free vote, the House rejected the proposal. There are good grounds for believing that had more than a mere 261 members voted, the decision would have gone the other way. One heard of many members who wanted a television experiment but who thought that their early departure from Westminster that whipless Thursday night would not cause the proposal to be rejected in the division lobbies. Unfortunately they did not foresee that Mr Richard Crossman, the then Leader of the House, would devote so much of his speech to a brilliant attack on the proposal he was supposed to be advocating.

The Commons television experiment has never taken place. In 1968 their lordships were more adventurous, though the closed-circuit experiment in the Lords proved only what should have been obvious: that it was no guide whatever on the question of televising the Commons.

For a time it looked as though the Commons might at least be bold enough to permit radio coverage. A closed-circuit radio experiment was permitted in the spring of 1968. A sub-committee of a committee then recommended edited radio coverage of Commons' proceedings. But the committee rejected this proposal on the grounds that financial reasons precluded expenditure 'on a project which is known to be controversial'. Although one finds it difficult to think of any new project costing public money which is not controversial, this was the justification given for postponing the opportunity to start the broadcasting of Parliament in the most inexpensive and least obtrusive way.

So after ten years, where are we? The present Leader of the House, Mr Fred Peart, approaches the issue with what he calls 'typical British caution'. But, with typical British daring, he adds: 'The door is not closed.' If this is so, the hinges are remarkably stiff. Only recently, it will be recalled, Mr Peart was immovably hostile to a unanimous request by the Select Committee on Race Relations that its public hearings outside Westminster should be open to television.

New objections may now be cited to justify delaying still further the broadcasting of Parliament, either in sound or vision. The cost of everything, especially television, is increasing. Both the BBC and independent television have their own financial problems. Any new charge to the Exchequer will be challenged. The advent of colour television may raise new questions of expense, and new technical problems to be surmounted. All of which will make the case for televising Parliament no easier to put. Yet that case, as the history of the past decade demonstrates, has become stronger every year.

If Parliament seeks to maintain its democratic authority at a time when all authority, however civilized, is under attack, would not television help to give it new influence and vitality? What Mr Aneurin Bevan told Parliament ten years ago is infinitely more relevant now:

'. . . in these days when all the apparatus of mass suggestion are against democratic education we should seriously consider re-establishing intelligent communication between the House of Commons and the electorate as a whole. That, surely, is a democratic process.'

If Parliament is increasingly regarded as too remote from the people, especially from the younger generation, television would help to bring it closer.

If Parliament is misunderstood, television would help to explain it.

If Parliament is slow to reform its ways, exposure to wider public view might help to accelerate this process. I do not go as far as the senior Cabinet Minister who said to me recently: 'If Parliament were televised it would be reformed overnight.' But is it unreasonable to suppose that the more informed public interest which would be stimulated by television in Parliament would in turn stimulate the movement towards parliamentary reform and modernization?

If parliamentary protest and criticism is being overshadowed by outside pressure groups, the televising of Parliament would help to communicate, and at the same time to reinforce the ways in which Parliament, in spite of all the jibes, is this country's central platform for democratic protest and enquiry.

If Parliament is getting weaker as the executive grows stronger, television would help to strengthen the influence of Parliament against the despotism of the state.

If Parliament is to develop its powers of control and scrutiny by committee, television coverage of such hearings might perform a valuable democratic and educative function. American television's coverage of the Fulbright hearings on foreign policy are a case in point which many British viewers have been able to see, and which some British MPs have envied.

If politicans complain, with justice, that television's treatment of politics is trivial and inadequate then an obvious remedy (as Mr Crossman pointed out with irresistible logic in his Granada lecture) is for the politicians to allow television to transmit their work in Parliament— not only by selected extracts, but by occasional 'live' and unedited broadcasts of those parliamentary events which are as important in politics as the Cup Final in sport.

If politics on television tends to be dominated by government (owing to government's inherent capacity to make news and create issues) then the televising of Parliament would show opposition criticism (together with that of party rebels and minorities) in a much more immediate and regular manner, and in daily juxtaposition with government.

If television's own interviews and discussions are thought sometimes to usurp the functions of parliamentary enquiry and debate, television from the House of Commons would enable the viewing public to see their rulers challenged and questioned by those elected for the purpose. The dangers, real or imagined, of interviews by television journalists, would thereby be reduced.

If Parliament is anxious to demonstrate its contemporary relevance why should it want to limit television coverage to occasions of medieval ceremony which, however delightful and splendid, do not exactly convey an impression of business-like modernity? By all means keep and show the pageantry. But let the people also see their Parliament at work.

All these arguments are immeasurably stronger in 1969 than in 1959. In putting them forward I am not concerned primarily with the interests of television, which is simply a means of communication, but with the interests of Parliament, which is the heart of our democratic system. Unfortunately Parliament has not always been able to see where its true interests lie. How would modern parliamentary government have developed without the press reporting which Parliament fought so long to prevent?

With regard to television, the fundamental issue can be seen now even more clearly than it could ten years ago. How can Parliament expect to maintain its prestige and authority as the nation's prime forum of debate if it continues to shut itself off from the nation's prime medium of mass communication?

Or as a Conservative parliamentarian once put it so aptly: 'Parliament must work with the tools of the age or it will sculpt no monument for the future.'

PART IV
Personal Flashback

Introduction

Though the publication of this book was timed to mark my twenty years in television I have put the emphasis on reflection rather than reminiscence. This is partly because the memories of journalists, especially those in television, are liable to seem as stale and insignificant as the ephemeral headlines which were so dramatic at the time. I have preferred reflection also because we are at a critical time in the history of our country—a time, especially where television is concerned, when we should be drawing lessons for the future rather than telling stories of the past.

I have therefore denied, or spared, the reader a narrative account of those fifteen years of my television career which have passed since my first book, *Television—a Personal Report*, in 1961. It would depress me, as I am sure it would depress my readers, if I were to exhume from their burial place amid the piles of yellowing press-cuttings, those moments on the screen which may have once had their transient impact, but which serve only as a reminder of

> '... old, unhappy, far-off things
> And battles long ago.'

Looking back I sometimes see nothing but a long receding vista of programme after programme, interview after interview, on endlessly recurring themes: the decline of British power, the Common Market, incomes policies, immigration, strikes, Vietnam, crime, Ulster, rows in the Labour Party, Ted Heath under attack, Liberal revivals and so on.

This is a somewhat unfair perspective because every occasion had its own interest and importance; and every programme may have made some contribution to public understanding. It was a period which has seen five General Elections (1964, 1966, 1970 and two in 1974) and a Referendum, when we, the broadcasters, did our best to illuminate the issues and probe the personalities. There were dozens of party conferences, budgets galore, and crisis after crisis, in all of which the television journalist tried to add his extra dimension to the press coverage. For most of the time politics centred on two leaders, Harold Wilson and Edward Heath. Future historians will be able to watch hour upon hour of videotaped interviews done with them by myself and others. Then there were the political mavericks whose massive personalities never failed to bring the screen alive: Enoch Powell, Quintin Hailsham, George Brown. There was the political turmoil in America, which finally led to Watergate. I think of those fantastic Presidential Conventions: Goldwater's in San Francisco in 1964, Mayor Daley's at Chicago in 1968, Nixon's at Miami in 1972.

But the hundreds of programmes which I have done have not been exclusively concerned with politics. For these were the years of heart transplants and moon-landings, of upheaval in the Catholic Church and revolt among students, of women's lib and the 'permissive' society. Until 1972 my work was mainly done in *Panorama*, but also in a host of other programmes (some now dead—like *Gallery* so regrettably axed in 1965, and 24 *Hours*), *Talk-in*, *Sunday Debate*, *Newsday*, *Daytime*, *People to Watch*, *University Forums*, *Election Forums*, campaign reports, election specials, strike specials, crisis specials, budget specials. Through the haze of recollection it is hard to focus on particular moments, and when I am asked to pick out the most important or the most exciting my mind invariably goes blank. But of course there were programmes or interviews which I do not forget and which stand out as remarkable for one reason or another.

Perhaps the most politically revealing was my interview with the 14th Earl of Home (as he then was) at Blackpool in 1963, when he refused four times to say if he was a candidate for the Tory leadership—in a way which made it very clear that he was.

The most hilarious: a heated exchange with George Brown during the 1964 Election Results Programme, which ended happily with my asking: 'May I call you brother?'

The most fascinating: almost any interview with Enoch Powell, especially the one where we discussed the 'arsenals of divine revenge' in which, apparently, the Almighty was storing weapons for use on Enoch's side in the political battle.

The most difficult: interviewing Ted Heath at No. 10 only a few minutes after the publication of a complicated Counter-Inflation Bill which he knew backwards.

The most impossible: an interview in which Jim Callaghan decides to mix it, whatever you try to ask.

The most unnerving: the interview with the former *Panorama* reporter Jan (née James) Morris about her change of sex.

The most bizarre: when Jomo Kenyatta acted as my interpreter in a *Panorama* interview with a somewhat unbalanced Mau-Mau General at Kenya's independence in 1963.

The most sensational: my long interview with Lord Lambton following his resignation after the Norma Levy scandal: 'People sometimes like variety' ... 'Taking opium in China is totally different from taking opium in Berwick-on-Tweed'.

The most ugliest and most distasteful: a tie between interviewing Sheik Karume of Zanzibar, and 'Bull' Connor, the police chief of Birmingham, Alabama.

The most moving: an interview with a very sick and very courageous RAF officer, the late Flight-Lieutenant Peter Dutton, who was waiting and hoping for a second kidney transplant after one that had failed.

The most depressing: the shocking exhibition of mindless pandemonium, physical threats, and screamed obscenities which was indulged in during two of my *University Forum* programmes by people receiving higher education.

The most stupid: a programme with an American lady who advocated childless marriage.

The most enjoyable: a televised speech I made in honour of Eric Morecambe and Ernie Wise. Even the ranks of Tuscany, including Eddie Braben, could scarce forbear to laugh.

Others may have their own recollections. I can only hope that the prevailing impression will be of someone who did his best to help his fellow citizens by searching for the truth which is undiscoverable, by explaining the inexplicable, and by trying to achieve the impossible—that standard of fairness which will satisfy even the most prejudiced.

As in any personal retrospect, when I look back at twenty years in television the events and excitements which are still most vividly in my mind are the early ones and in particular those surrounding my entry into television in 1955. So here in Part IV of this book are reprinted extracts from the account I wrote in 1961 about what it was like to be in at the beginning of ITN, the breaking of the BBC monopoly, and the birth of the new electronic journalism in the 1950s, twenty years ago.

Those events were recent and familiar when these chapters first appeared.[1] Many who read them for the first time now, fifteen years later, may find them interesting for the very opposite reason—namely that they are contemporary descriptions of what now seems strange, distant and almost primitive in television. These chapters show, I hope, something of the enthusiasm and excitement which gripped everyone who, in the mid-'fifties, was involved in creating the new journalism and the new dimension of democracy which television made possible.

The fame (or notoriety) achieved by appearing on television is artificial. It is wildly disproportionate to the social contribution made by those who so appear. But for good or ill if you are on that box, in millions of homes for twenty years, you get to be known as an individual to people in a way that no other medium has ever made possible. Whether they like you or hate you, they feel they know you and they want to know more about you. So Part IV also includes for a new generation of viewers and readers, the story of how I came to enter television just at the moment it was about to explode with massive force, shattering many old conventions and taboos and creating many new dangers and problems.

[1]In *Television: A Personal Report* (Hutchinson) 1961.

1. Opportunity

To this account of how my luck turned, I would like to add something which I did not know of until long after I wrote this chapter. In 1955 the first ITN newscaster auditions were played back to a critical audience of top ITV executives. Mine was not popular. I was definitely not what they thought they wanted. In the end I was offered the job only because Aidan Crawley threatened to resign if he, as Editor, was not allowed to engage me. So it is to him that I owe my opportunity in television, even more than I ever realized.

The newscaster audition described in this chapter cannot have provided any overwhelming evidence to justify his insistence. All I know is that he was looking for someone who was clear, forceful and above all genuinely interested.

So I can only suppose that a flicker of these qualities must have been conveyed to him, if to no one else, by that audition of mine twenty years ago. But I would hate to see it now.

One hot afternoon in June 1955 the telephone rang in my small office on the second floor of Broadcasting House, where I was working as a producer of topical radio programmes.

The call was from an old friend, Ronald Waterhouse.[1] We had been called to the Bar together in February 1952. Unlike me, Waterhouse had stayed in practice. He knew that since leaving the Bar I had not found the job I wanted and was not content to remain a BBC radio producer. He was telephoning to tell me about a job he had seen advertised at lunch-time that day. It was pinned up on the notice board of Gray's Inn—along with notices of other jobs open to barristers and law students. 'I thought you might be interested in this one,' he said.

'Go on,' I replied, without much enthusiasm, thinking it was one of the usual humdrum jobs in government or commerce offered to young barristers who are unable to keep going at the Bar. But I listened, just in case.

[1] Now Ronald Waterhouse, QC.

'Independent Television News Limited invites applications for the post of "newscaster".'

What exactly did that mean?

'The job would involve helping to prepare, and appearing on the screen to deliver, the daily news bulletins for the new Independent Television service due to start next autumn.'

This sounded more interesting than I had expected. I wanted to hear more. I suggested to my secretary that it was a convenient moment for her to go for tea. This telephone conversation was not one which should be overheard in Broadcasting House.

The summer of 1955 was a time of tense and conspiratorial excitement in the broadcasting world. BBC staff were being secretly approached with lucrative offers. For the first time since the birth of radio in 1922, when Mr John Reith became first General Manager of the British Broadcasting 'Company', employees of the BBC had the chance of an alternative career in broadcasting. Nowhere was this prospect regarded as more evil and dangerous than in Broadcasting House, the great building in Portland Place shaped like the stern of an ocean liner, the shrine dedicated for so many years to the ideal of public-service broadcasting.

No longer were the professional hopes of BBC staff limited by the roneoed notices displayed in the corridors of 'B.H.':

'Vacancy for a talks producer Grade B1 minus starting at such and such, rising by five annual increments of £50 to a maximum of so much.'

There were vacancies in every branch of the Corporation, but all within the elaborate structure of this mammoth monopoly, with its carefully graded hierarchy, its formal selection boards, and its cautious system of promotion.

From time to time the notice boards would carry details of the BBC's next television training course, offering a glimpse of that strange Bohemian world on the other side of London in the dingy street called Lime Grove, from which were beginning to come rumours of new ideas and rumbling rebellion against the dead hand of Broadcasting House. Admittedly, I had been only too pleased indeed relieved, when BBC radio had given me a temporary contract as a producer earlier that year. It was a job for the like of which hundreds regularly applied. But even if I could get on to the permanent staff, which seemed unlikely, steam radio did not inspire me as a career. I had tried, and failed, to get a BBC television course.

So to a lowly radio producer, on a temporary BBC contract, the possibility of a job with the new commercial television network was intensely exciting. With my secretary safely out of earshot, I listened avidly to the rest of the ITN advertisement.

'No previous broadcasting experience necessary.'

As it happened, I could claim quite a bit.

'Requirements: sound knowledge of current affairs, ability to think on feet, good presence.'

Well, I thought, that's put pretty broadly. No harm in trying.

'The work might appeal to a barrister thinking of giving up practice. The post would carry a good salary.'

But for my friend Ronald Waterhouse, I would never have known of this advertisement which was aimed at the Bar; as a BBC radio producer, I had lost contact with that profession.

I had heard very little of ITN, except that it had just been formed by the new commercial companies to provide their network news service, and that a former Labour MP, Aidan Crawley, who had established himself as a TV commentator in his BBC series *Viewfinder*, had been appointed editor.

But I did not hesitate for a single moment. Here was obviously a chance to move into something new and big, into a job where my legal background and interest in current affaires could apparently be put to good use. By the time my secretary returned from tea, I had already written a letter of application. From my briefcase I took a list of my qualifications and experience. For speed in applying for jobs I used at that time to keep several typed copies ready to enclose with letters of application:

'Age 32 ... BBC current affairs radio producer ... Various free-lance broadcasts and articles ... Served Royal Artillery 1943-7 ... Studied Law at Oxford 1947-51 ... President of the Oxford Union Society 1950 ... called to the Bar 1952, practised till 1953 ... Press officer with British Information Services in Washington 1953-4 ... Joined BBC radio 1955 ...'

This was enclosed with a covering letter to the deputy-editor of ITV, Richard Goold-Adams, previously on *The Economist* and a regular BBC broadcaster. The letter was in the post within an hour. An interview followed a few days later with Goold-Adams and ITN's senior producer, James Bredin, who had produced Aidan Crawley's BBC series *Viewfinder*. Then came an audition. That summer scores of would-be newscasters were going in a steady stream for five-minute tests at a closed-circuit TV studio in Hampstead; ITN's own Kingsway studio was not yet in operation. Names were weeded down to a short list of six. I was one.

ITN's final newscaster auditions were held in a closed-circuit studio in Highbury. Not being sure where the place was, I arrived much too early at Finsbury Park tube station. At a wine-merchant's I bought one of those very small bottles of brandy. I walked to a Lyons tea-shop in the Seven Sisters Road. Sitting at a table in the tea-shop, I hoped no one would notice me take the bottle from my pocket and pour the brandy into a cup. It seemed an odd thing to be doing on a sweltering July day. I don't usually feel the need for a drink at a moment of stress. On this occasion I felt a definite need for the fortifying comfort, real or imaginary, of hard liquor. . . .

Slowly sipping from that cup of brandy in a Lyons tea-shop in the Seven Sisters Road, I read and re-read the notes of the 'dummy' newscast we had been instructed to prepare. It had to cover the main points of the previous evening's news—about four minutes' material. The items were to be given straight through, one after the other—not interspersed with film as they would be in a real TV bulletin. It was simply a test of newscasting, with only the spoken items which a news-caster would ordinarily give to introduce film, or to report news for which there was no film, such as a court case or a Commons debate.

We had been sent a summary of the news and told to put it into our own style, choosing our own order of items. The only requirements from Aidan Crawley were that the facts should be clear and that the style should try to combine the responsibility of the *Manchester Guardian* and the vigour of the *Daily Express*! This was aiming wide and high—typical of Aidan Crawley's approach. This tall, rugged man, with his jutting chin and warm, expansive manner, exuded energy and optimism.

At the gate leading into the recording studio I was surprised to meet a well-known journalist from the *Sunday Times*, Mr Cyril Ray, whom I knew as a contributor to the BBC programmes on which I was a producer. We were both slightly embarrassed at meeting. He was one of the final six and had just been tested, so he knew what I was doing there. I begged him not to breathe a word to my superiors at Broadcasting House. As I later discovered, this would not have done my position with the BBC any harm—rather the reverse. He told me how his test had gone. 'Bloody,' he said.

Inside the studio the atmosphere was more tense and operational that at the first test in Hampstead, which had been a quick in-and-out business with no recording. Here, everything was set up for a 'take'. I was told to sit at a table a deliver my newscast straight into the lens of the camera. No one except two or three studio technicians was present. Aidan Crawley was in another room to watch the recording being made. The camera lined up its shot. The floor-manager explained the winding-up signals he would give me: '*one minute . . . thirty seconds . . . fifteen seconds . . . out*'. He told me to watch for these signals out of the corner of my eye without ever looking away from the camera. I was to end exactly on time. This was a vital point of the exercise. Fortunately my piece had been timed carefully. If I did it at a good, but not galloping, speed, it was reasonably certain to end on time.

A message was passed from Aidan Crawley that I was to speak to the camera as if it were a person sitting at home. The camera stood cold and inhuman ten feet away. At first I could hardly pick out the lens because I was dazzled by the fierce battery of lights blazing down upon me. After a few minutes my eyes adjusted themselves and I fixed my gaze on the small circle of thick glass, hooded by a black tube, like the end of a powerful telescope. It did not seem a very friendly object.

Yes, I said, I was ready to go. But there was a little more delay. The lighting was causing trouble with my spectacles—reflection flashes from the lenses and shadows from the heavy horn-rims. An engineer climbed up ladders to adjust the arc-lamps until the director in the control room was satisfied. It seemed to take a very long time. I began to sweat under the heat of the lights.

We had been asked to memorize our material so that we would not have to look down during the audition. They wanted to see us looking full-face into the camera as continuously as we could. I took a final look at my notes. The phrases which last night had seemed crisp and bright were limp and dull, but it was too late to make any more changes.

'Are you ready?' called the floor-manager, listening to the director's orders on his headphones. I nodded.

'Stand by.' He stood to one side of the camera, and raised his arm above his shoulder.

'Thirty seconds to go . . . Fifteen seconds.'

Suddenly the floor-manager jabbed his hand down towards me. A red light glowed on top of the camera. This was it.

Immediately I found that the last few seconds of studio tension had communicated itself to me. I felt a sudden burst of vitality and a compelling urge to give out the news items I had prepared. No longer did they seem stale or dreary. They were fresh, exciting, and charged with vital significance. I rapped out each item with a mounting sense of urgency and crisis. It must have sounded as if I was reporting the end of the world.

I ended dead on time. I flopped back against the chair. Though at this moment nothing was further from my mind, that working-up second by second, to the tense climax of transmission was to be part of my daily life during the next few years. Lights, cameras, clocks, signals, were to form the ritual setting for the culmination of a day's work.

'Mr Crawley says thank you very much.'

Aidan Crawley met me outside the studio. He was friendly and non-committal. My spectacles still bothered him. 'Could you get some lighter spectacles?' Crawley inquired.

'Of course,' I replied, sensing that he might still be interested. We shook hands and he promised to let me know.

Shortly afterwards, Aidan Crawley's secretary rang me at Broadcasting House with the cloak-and-dagger message: 'If you will come to see Mr Crawley tomorrow he will tell you something to your advantage.' I went, and he did.

That, in answer to the many people who have been kind enough to

ask. is how I began in television. I had no pull, no strings, no contacts.
I liked the look of the job with Aidan Crawley, and Aidan Crawley
liked the look of me—though for some time, as I will explain later, he
was one of the few people who did.

I was in no doubt about leaving my job in BBC radio. I had applied
unsuccessfully for work or training in BBC TV when I returned in
1954 after a year in America. I wrote to Leonard Miall, the newly
appointed Head of TV Talks whom I had known in Washington when
he was BBC news correspondent there. He referred me to his assistant,
Mrs Grace Wyndham Goldie, who very kindly saw me. She was unable to offer me anything in television, but commended me to the
attention of the sound-radio people. Three or four months passed,
during which I was desperately hard up. I did evening lectures for the
Workers' Educational Association at two guineas a time. Then the
Talks Department at Broadcasting House offered me free-lance work,
and eventually a temporary producer's contract on the programme *At
Home and Abroad* under its producer Stephen Bonarjee.

As soon as I received Aidan Crawley's offer to join ITN, I went to
inform the Head of my Department of my reason for leaving the
Corporation. Three weeks previously he had read out to me a somewhat tepid departmental report on my progress. Now, he immediately
became effusive. Holding up a bundle of files from his pending-tray,
he said: 'But your name is very high on the short lists for these vacancies
on our permanent staff—very high indeed.'

I replied that it was a bit late to tell me that. He then observed: 'I
suppose we aren't paying you very much?'

'No,' I said.

'Well, then,' said the Departmental Head, 'would it help if I were
to ask the Director-General for an immediate and special increase in
your salary?' I was practically struck dumb by this sudden interest towards someone who had battered at the BBC's doors for months. I
had a hilarious vision of General Sir Ian Jacob solemnly considering a
little memorandum headed: 'The Case of R. Day—Urgent', and
weighing in his precise mind the sum appropriate in the circumstances.
Suppressing my amusement, I managed to murmur something about
it being more a question of opportunity. This was true, because my
initial salary from ITN was to be hardly any more than my BBC pay.
I then brought the discussion to a head.

'What would you do if you were me?'

'Do you want me to answer personally or officially?'

'Personally,' I replied, hastily.

'I would go,' he said. 'It is obviously a big chance for you.' He was very nice about it and has been very friendly whenever we have met since.

A big chance, he had said. Yes—but a big challenge. Aidan Crawley had offered me only a three-month trial. I might be an abysmal flop. Everyone would know about it. The first efforts of commercial television were bound to come under a fierce spotlight of publicity. Criticism would be merciless. If ITN dropped me, what then? I could hardly go crawling back to the BBC for a nice safe job rising by increments of fifty pounds a year. But I was not in the mood for 'Safety First'. I would not be the only new boy. I would enjoy the work. I hoped to do it well. At least I would have a damn good try.

I was extremely fortunate to enter television journalism at this particular time. It was not just a new job in a new field. The mid-1950s ushered in a revolution in the social and political life of Britain. Since 1954 television has been spreading at the rate of over a million new homes each year. By 1962 there should be about 12 million television licence-holders. The 5-million mark was passed in 1955, and BBC television transmissions were then already within reach of 94 per cent of the population. In that year, as Britain was moving towards mass viewing on a nation-wide scale, the BBC television monopoly was broken.

Under the last administration of Sir Winston Churchill, Parliament had set up the Independent Television Authority 'to make provision for television broadcasting services in addition to those provided by the British Broadcasting Corporation'. ITV went on the air for the first time on September 22nd 1955. Not more than 200,000 homes were then equipped with sets that could get the new programme.

Six years later it is hard to realize how revolutionary was the coming of ITV. The BBC had achieved a position in British life which was apparently impregnable. The Government's decision to set up a rival television service, financed by commercial advertising, was taken in the teeth of violent opposition, some of it within the Conservative Party. The Establishment was split wide open. On one side was the Labour Party Front Bench, allied with Lord Hailsham, Lady Violet Bonham Carter, and *The Times*. On the other was the Conservative

Cabinet, supported by City interests who, urged on by Norman Collins[1] and others, were ready, willing, and able to risk their capital.

Ever since then commercial television has been endlessly debated. Parliament, press, and public have argued about the amount of advertising, the vast profits made by the programme contractors, the huge capital gains made by the few shrewd enough to gamble their money at the start, the quality of the programmes, the effect of ITV competition on the BBC, and the role of the Independent Television Authority. It is not my purpose to wade through the pros and cons of all these issues, but in the final chapter there are some suggestions for the future, a contribution to the debate accompanying the Pilkington inquiry.[2]

What I am concerned with is that in the last few years television has grown up into a supremely important medium of news and opinion. This is partly because of the mass audience, which has forced politicians, trade-union leaders, and other public figures to wake up to the potentialities of TV. It is also due to the spur of ITV competition. I do not suggest that no significant developments in this field took place before 1955. That would be unfair to the BBC and to those talented members of its staff, such as Mrs Grace Wyndham Goldie, who in the post-war decade were exploring the new territory of television technique and were trying to free television from the inhibitions and restrictions inherited from radio. But the fact is that some of the famous topical programmes for which the BBC has won high prestige did not come into being until after ITV started. *Tonight* did not begin until 1957. *Monitor* did not begin until 1958. *Face to Face* did not begin until 1959, a year after ITN had run the first regular series of lengthy interviews with eminent people. Take *Panorama*, now regarded as an old-established institution. *Panorama*, in its weekly form, was launched one week before ITV went on the air in September 1955, and did not get into its stride until ITV was under way. (An earlier version of *Panorama*, fortnightly, began two years earlier. According to an article in *The Listener* 'these two years do not really count'. Michael Barsley, a producer of the early *Panorama*, disagrees. He cites enterprising achievements in the 1953-5 period. Even so, *Panorama* was put under new management when it first appeared as a weekly review.) As regards news, it was not until long after ITN had won widespread praise for

[1]Former BBC executive, later deputy Chairman of ATV.
[2]The Pilkington Committee was set up in 1960 and published its report in 1962.

its vigour and freshness that the BBC Television News began to humanize itself.

So, while the BBC has won well-deserved praise for the high standard of these prestige programmes, it was the challenge of ITV that had spurred the Corporation to make better use of its able staff and resources. There were those who thought that ITV would force the BBC to lower its standards. On the contrary, though the BBC's rivals have concentrated on popular entertainment at peak hours, one remarkable effect (or sequel, at least) of commercial competition has been the vastly improved BBC coverage of serious topical matters. Another post-ITV development was the TV coverage of elections. New ground was broken at the Rochdale by-election in 1958 when Granada televised the three candidates. Extraordinary though it may now seem, the 1959 General Election was the first time that a campaign had been reported like any other news on television, and the first time that there were programmes with ordinary candidates in addition to the party broadcasts.

In other words, so far as news and current affairs were concerned' what happened in 1955 was that a great gust of fresh air blew into British television. The BBC, at first slightly stunned was enormously invigorated, and hit back boldly. The Corporation quickly bought up ITV's first big star personality, Chris Chataway, who had been my colleague as one of ITN's first newscasters. Chris was taken on by *Panorama* in May 1956. Later on, as a counter-attack provoked by ITV's decision to break the 'toddlers' truce' between six and seven in the evening, the programme *Tonight* was hurriedly launched. Some of the BBC's talented young producers like Donald Baverstock (*Tonight*) and Michael Peacock (*Panorama*) had their salaries jacked up under personal contracts to prevent them from leaving the Corporation. When ITV started, many BBC people in both radio and television had seized the chance to move over. Some of these had already made a name in the BBC. Others were unknown people who had been unable to find an opening in BBC television. I was one of the latter.

2. Roads which led to TV

The significance of this chapter is that unlike so many of the younger people now in television I did not come into it in my early twenties with nothing behind me but school and university. I was thirty-two. After four and a half years in the Army I did not go up to Oxford until I was nearly twenty-four. Television never entered my head at that time, but the next few years happened to be spent in a variety of activities which were to prove a useful background when I began in television.

Those who enter television too young are apt to be too impressed by television's values and too obsessed by its techniques. It is television which has the impact on them, not the other way round.

I had had my first taste of journalism as an undergraduate. I was a 'stringer' (local free-lance reporter) in Oxford for the American magazine *Time*. I had met Miss Honor Balfour, *Time*'s expert on British politics, when she was writing a feature about Oxford. The magazine happened to need a stringer in the University, and I was sent various assignments. *Time* had an insatiable interest in Oxford happenings, from undergraduate pranks to the eccentricities of dons whose prestige as egg-heads appeared to be greater over there than over here. The money for these jobs was a welcome addition to my ex-serviceman's grant.

I would telephone my material to *Time*'s London office in Bond Street. It was rarely recognizable when the story appeared a week or two later. 'Copy' for *Time* is rewritten in New York into the magazines special brand of slick, condensed journalese.

But I sent them one story that ran largely verbatim for a column and a half. They did not need to soup it up. It was a report of a hot-tempered Oxford Union debate, over which I presided, between Randolph Churchill and Professor Joad. The debate was on the motion (backed by Joad) 'That this House regrets the influence of America as the leading democratic power'. A choice 'quote' was Churchill's reference to Joad (who had recently been in court for travelling 'First' without paying the proper fare) as 'a third-class Socrates'. That report earned me fifteen guineas, which made me wonder for the first time about the possibility of earning a living in journalism. This was no more than a passing thought, because I was still optimistically intent on the Bar.

Parliament? Yes, this was always a cherished ambition, but, being then an obstinate Liberal,[1] I was under no illusions. In any case, I believed it was foolish to think about standing for parliament until one could claim some kind of experience to justify Parliamentary candidature.

I spoke regularly in Union debates, and kept abreast of politics and current events. The traditional settings of debates at the Oxford and Cambridge Unions have become familiar in recent years to radio and television audiences. On a dais sit the President and his officers in full evening dress. On the benches are the 'honourable members'. Procedure is formal, in parliamentary style, with adjournments, points of order, and votes of 'no confidence'. In the Oxford Union the debating hall is lined with busts and paintings of men who were elected President in their undergraduate days—such as Gladstone, Asquith, F. E. Smith, William Temple, Hilaire Belloc, John Simon. The latest piece of sculpture is a bust of Harold Macmillan, who just missed the Presidency; his university career was interrupted in August 1914.

On a big night the debating hall is packed with undergraduates on the floor and their girl-friends in the gallery. Distinguished guests come to speak in the debates, and sometimes get a rough reception. The undergraduate audience is critical, hoping for something better than hackneyed argument and stale wit. After the main speeches the undergraduates pour out of the hall to drink at the bar. Only a few are left behind—mainly those who wish to speak. In this frigid atmosphere the aspiring Union speaker finds it a severe challenge to his courage, let alone eloquence, to address the handful of yawning cynical undergraduates scattered about the empty hall. If he passes this test he gets his chance as a main speaker, with an audience of seven or eight hundred.

For a young man wishing to try his hand at the art of public speaking, the University offers no better platform. He debates in public with

[1]Since 1959, when I stood for Parliament as a Liberal, I have not been a Liberal Party supporter and have had no party allegiance.

Cabinet Ministers and leading parliamentarians. He learns to cope with hecklers and keep his temper. For someone who comes, as I did, from a small college, the Union is an invaluable way of meeting a wide circle of undergraduates.

Among the Union Presidents in my generation were Sir Edward Boyle, Anthony Wedgwood Benn, Peter Kirk, and Jeremy Thorpe, all of whom are now Members of Parliament. Then there was Kenneth Tynan, Union Secretary in 1949. Tynan was a legendary undergraduate figure with his purple suit, his ghostly pale face, and incredibly long hair reaching down outside his coat-collar. He was a brilliant, uncanny performer, transforming an awkward stammer into an asset which kept the audience on tenterhooks. He never failed to pack the debating hall.

For those interested in politics and current events there was a stream of Ministers, Opposition leaders and back-bench personalities visiting the University to debate at the Union or to address the political clubs. Nowadays it is not only undergraduates who have the frequent opportunity to see debated between leading protagonists on the political scene. Thanks to television, the most popular visiting performers in my time at Oxford (such as Boothby, Crossman, and Michael Foot) have since become familiar to an audience far wider than the few who go to a university or attend ordinary political meetings. The topical debates which traditionally have been the thought-provoking pastime of university students have their mass counterpart in the TV age, through the televising of forthright discussions and provocative interviews. As Mr Henry Fairlie has put it: 'Whatever else television may have done, it has introduced into every home in the country the habit of listening to argument.'

My desultory studies of the Law were interrupted in 1949 by a three-month trip to the United States. This was my first visit to America and gave me my first experience of television. I was chosen as one of a two-man debating team to represent the Oxford Union. My companion was Geoffrey Johnson Smith, who was then a Labour Party supporter. At the end of our trip he took a job in San Francisco and married an attractive American psychiatrist. He is now a Conservative and became MP for Holborn and St Pancras.[1]

Our tour took us to about fifty universities, colleges, and academies,

[1]Since 1965, MP for East Grinstead.

including Yale, Columbia, and Chicago, and the service academies at West Point and Annapolis. We went to huge state universities in Virginia and Illinois and to small colleges like Wabash College, Wabash, Indiana; a different place every night, with a hectic travel-schedule by plane, train, and Greyhound bus.

The Americans took their debating very seriously. Most of those with whom we debated were studying for a Degree in Speech. We were surprised to find Professors of Forensics, Coaches of Debate, and Faculties of Speech. Debates were concluded by an elaborate system of judging. Points would be awarded for various aspects of oratorical technique: logic, 'argumentation', style, presentation, humour, persuasiveness, and even gestures. At the University of Illinois a member of the Faculty came up to me and said: 'Those gestures of yours were terrific. I made a very careful note of them.' At one college points were also awarded for dress. Fortunately, Johnson Smith was always immaculate.

This debating tour was an invaluable experience. What with the war and the dollar restrictions, very few of my generation had ever been to America. To us it was a glittering land of plenty at a time when 'austerity' Britain was struggling hard to recover from the war effort.

Between debates we saw the sights, visited the homes of our hosts, and went to the ball games. We talked to rotary clubs and businessmen's luncheons, and were interviewed on radio and television. It was in Philadelphia, in October 1949, that I first appeared before a television camera. Like so many American TV programmes, this one was informal to the point of chaos. The interviewer had not the slightest idea who we were or why we were on his show. We wandered into the studio and then wandered out again after a rambling and incoherent interview that cannot have been of the slightest interest or amusement to the worthy inhabitants of Philadelphia—except possibly when the interviewer mimicked our English accents very badly.

Apart from meeting students, we met several eminent Americans, including Mrs Eleanor Roosevelt and General Eisenhower. Mrs Roosevelt kindly invited us to lunch at her home at Hyde Park, near New York. She chatted endlessly about her husband, about the great people she had met when she was living at the White House. I recall her quoting a remark made by President Roosevelt about Churchill during the war. 'The trouble with Winston,' F.D.R. had said, 'is that he enjoyed the old world too much to understand the new.'

At that time General Eisenhower was President of Columbia University. We had debated with some Columbia students and he offered to see us. He asked us what subjects we had been debating. He was interested to hear that one of our topics was public ownership of basic industries. 'Y'know,' said Ike, 'I've just set up a panel of the finest brains here in Columbia to work on this very issue—in an entirely non-political way, of course.' The General spoke crisply and confidently. 'I have asked them to *draw the line* between public and private enterprise.' I suggested that this might not be so very simple and that a slump, for instance, might require special Government action. Ike paused for a second. 'Oh, sure,' he said, 'it won't be a *straight* line.'

Those exciting three months in America were soon over. I was back in Oxford with the shadow of the final examinations looming ahead. Somewhat mistakenly I had chosen to read Law. I would have done better to have taken a degree in some broader, less vocational subject like History or P.P.E. (Politics, Philosophy, and Economics). I could not work up much interest in academic legal studies. The intricacies of our Common Law, traced back through centuries of precedent, form an abstruse body of learning all on their own. Our Land Law, for instance, has been aptly described as 'a lumber-room of medieval pedantry'. I am afraid I was more interested in advocacy and cross-examination than in arid legal principles. I hoped that, once I was in practice, the principles that seemed so remote in a library would quickly come to life when applied to a problem with which one was personally confronted.

I did not stay long enough at the Bar to know whether this hope was justified. My friends were surprised when I decided to leave. I had been awarded one of the Middle Temple's Harmsworth Scholarships of £200 a year for three years. My earnings were good compared with those of other newly called barristers. Without any solicitor connections (which never help much anyway) I earned 200 guineas in my pupil year. Most of all, I was lucky enough to be a pupil of Mr F. H. Lawton, who later became a judge of the High Court.[1] He appeared in many celebrated trials. He defended Guenther Podola in 1959.

Lawton's practice took him into every type of court. I went with him

[1]Since 1972 the Rt. Hon. Sir Frederick Lawton, Lord Justice of Appeal.

to Bow Street, to the Old Bailey, to Assizes and Quarter Sessions on the South-Eastern circuit, and to the Law Courts in the Strand. As Fred Lawton's pupil, I read his briefs and took notes behind him in court. It was a fascinating experience to watch a successful advocate at work, and to study his technique of cross-examination. Other barristers appearing in big cases which I attended as a pupil or with a 'noting' brief were Sir Hartley Shawcross and Mr Gerald Gardiner, who were then two brilliant advocates at the top of their profession. I was able to watch their work at close quarters.

I began to get a little work of my own, with the smaller cases which used to come into Lawton's chambers, at two or three guineas a time. These would include minor crimes (driving offences, petty theft, etc.) and small County Court cases. One type of case, often given to the newly called barrister, would be to make a plea in mitigation of sentence in a case where the accused had pleaded guilty. This looks a simple matter in court—but I found it terribly difficult. I remember racking my brains to find anything to say on behalf of a man who had pleaded guilty to his eighth conviction for robbery with violence. In the end the only thing I could find to say to the judge was: 'Your Lordship will note that my client has used rather less violence on this occasion than he has in the past.' I was sick with nerves. The judge, Mr Justice Hilbery, was a senior judge who was capable of being very difficult. He looked sour as I made my little speech in Court No. 1 at the Old Bailey. When I sat down he said grudgingly to the man in the dock, who must have been very disappointed with his counsel: 'Mr Day has said the only possible thing that can be said on your behalf,' and then gave him five years.

There were more satisfying moments, when one's client was acquitted in spite of what had at first seemed a strong prosecution case. I was particularly proud to have persuaded a Bench of magistrates to dismiss a charge of indecent exposure against a lorry driver. It was a minor case, but to this young working man, with his pretty wife, a terrible one. The couple went away with a nasty shadow lifted from their lives. I felt, for once, that I had earned my two-guinea fee—and more.

Although fees were beginning to trickle in, I did not think I could stand the Bar much longer. I was now twenty-nine, having been four years at Oxford after leaving the Army. With average luck I might hope to earn a very moderate living by the time I was thirty-five. After

The BBC's 1964 General Election Results coverage

With Sir Hugh Greene and Miss Joan Marsden at 1964 General Election rehearsal

HRH Princess Anne presenting Robin Day with the Richard Dimbleby Award, February 26th 19

During a long election night stint

paying for rent of chambers, rail fares, hotel expenses, and legal text-books, the five or six pounds a week I was earning in fees was reduced to nothing. At the age of twenty-nine this was a miserable situation. Even if I could stick it out a bit longer, with the aid of my Middle Temple Scholarship and by earning money in other ways, did I really want to stay at the Bar?

I had begun to doubt whether I wanted to live the life of a busy barrister. I did not believe I would ever acquire that professional detachment which would enable me to bear the strain of a barrister's life. I used to go through agonies of doubt and depression about cases which I handled, particularly those of a squalid and tragic nature. I felt oppressed by the dated, class-conscious atmosphere which pervaded the Law, and which from time to time is revealed to the public in a highly publicized case. ('Is it a book,' asked *Lady Chatterley's* prosecutor, 'that you would even wish your wife or your servants to read?')

Finally, even if I could build up a reasonable knock-about practice as an advocate, I did not believe I had that peculiar type of intellectual ability which goes to make a good lawyer. After a long period of un-certainty that lasted throughout the summer of Coronation year, I decided to leave the Bar.

I did not regard my time at the Bar as wasted. A knowledge of the courts and the principles of our Common Law was an invaluable background from any standpoint. The ordeal of the first few appearances in court had been a toughening experience. Television has never been as nerve-racking. From my pupillage with F. H. Lawton I had learned the simple but often neglected lesson that a good cross-examination depends on thorough mastery of the subject, and on the ability to anticipate almost any answer. I was certain that somewhere, somehow, I would be able to make good use of those eighteen months in the Temple. I could not for the life of me see either where or how. Tele-vision never crossed my mind. Fleet Street attracted me, but a few inquiries showed that editors, somewhat understandably, weren't very interested in giving jobs to out-of-work barristers. All I could offer, apart from Oxford and the Bar, were one or two articles I had written for the press.

I did not want to drift into a business office or a Government depart-ment as a 'legal eagle' with all the tedium, and none of the excitement, of the Bar. I had no further use for my black coat and striped trousers.

I sold my wig and gown to a friend[1] and made a clean break with the Law.

So in September 1953, without any idea of how the future would work out, I went to America. The chance of a job in the United States arose from my undergraduate debating tour four years previously. At that time I had met the late Charles Campbell, head of the Washington office of British Information Services. He had heard me speak before a large audience at a Washington university in 1949. Campbell was a legendary figure among journalists on both sides of the Atlantic. He was British-born, but had lived almost all his life in America. His very British appearance (florid face, military moustache) concealed a shrewd understanding and deep love of America. If any man earned the nickname 'Mr Anglo-American' it was Charlie Campbell. He was looking for a young assistant in his job of dealing with Washington's press, radio, and TV. It was not a permanent job and was poorly paid, in the locally recruited category. This meant I had to pay my own passage to America and be appointed there. I had left the Bar before running completely out of cash, in order to tide me over the period of looking for new work. I had just enough for the transatlantic passage. It was a wild and impulsive thing to do.

There was no career in the post I was taking and I couldn't keep chopping and changing jobs much longer. But I longed to know more about America. There was a chance that a year or so in Washington would widen my background and lead me on to something else. One part of the job was to be liaison officer with Washington TV and radio stations. I was to study the programmes, particularly those which might feature British visitors or spokesmen. It turned out to be a useful year. I made speaking tours in parts of America I had not visited before and broadcast on local radio and TV stations. I got to know some of the leading journalists in Washington, and watched the way they covered the news.

American politics were going through a shameful phase. McCarthyism was at its height. For weeks in the summer of 1954 I watched the famous Army-McCarthy hearings which were televised daily through-

---

[1]Ivan Yates, of the *Observer*, who was killed in a car accident in February 1975. Though he was never called to the Bar, he kept my wig and gown safely, and presented them to my wife when she was called in 1968.

out America. Television may have helped Senator McCarthy's rise to fame, but it helped to kill him in the end. The American people were able to see him (and his callow associates Cohn and Schine) exposed by the subtle but deadly questioning of the Army's lawyer Joseph Welch. Never have I seen a more dramatic moment on television than when Welch turned to McCarthy after the Senator had made an utterly unjustified smear about the student activities of one of Welch's Harvard assistants. This had nothing to do with the hearings. It was a sickening example of McCarthy's technique which had terrorized America's Government and horrified her friends throughout the world. This time the Senator did not go unanswered. Joseph Welch, the courteous Boston lawyer with the old-world manner, voiced the feeling of millions watching. He turned on McCarthy with a cold fury and a noble eloquence:

'Until this moment, Senator, I think I had never gauged your cruelty or your recklessness.... If it were in my power to forgive you for your reckless cruelty, I would do so. I like to think that I am a gentle man, but your forgiveness will have to come from someone other than me.'

The devastating contempt with which these words were delivered cannot be appreciated from the printed record. The power of television has served America ill in many ways, but the nation-wide transmission of Welch's rejoinder to McCarthy will stand to its lasting credit in the balance-sheet of television history.

An outstanding event of that year in Washington was Sir Winston Churchill's last visit to America as Prime Minister. I had some duties connected with the press arrangements. It never occurred to me that I would meet the great man, but I was detailed to attend a private briefing which Sir Winston gave to British correspondents. The small gathering of newsmen waited in the sunshine on the garden steps of the British Embassy in Massachusetts Avenue. The old man came walking slowly out through the French windows, steadying himself with his walking-stick. He was then seventy-nine. After his stroke earlier in the year the gruelling round of talks in the Washington heat had left him exhausted. But he beamed broadly as he shook hands with each of us. Then Sir Winston began to speak, gravely, yet with just the hint of a mischievous twinkle in his eye. I treasure the memory of his opening remark to the eagerly assembled journalists, who were hanging on his every word: 'Gentlemen, I hope you will permit me to take up a few minutes of your valuable time . . .'

My year in Washington went quickly. The summer, especially, was a continual round of those parties which are such an exhausting feature of the American capital. Diplomats, politicians, journalists, officials, drink one another's cocktails on the shaded patios of Georgetown, Washington's old and elegant residential quarter. On a gayer level were those energetic party-givers, the young lawyers and State Department men from Harvard and Yale, with their lavatory-brush haircuts, their narrow-shouldered seersucker suits, and their dates—bright, clean, neat, eager American girls. It was fun for a while, but I was intent on returning home to find a new career. My thoughts now centred on journalism and broadcasting. I had tried to learn everything I could from the newspapermen and commentators I had got to know in Washington. Charlie Campbell and others had given me letters of introduction. Broadcasting seemed my best bet. From the British newspapers, and from letters written by friends in London, it was clear that a new field of opportunities in British broadcasting was now opening. That summer Parliament had passed the Television Act, to launch commercial television.

It looked like a good time to try my luck, first with the BBC, and when the commercial people started the following year I might try them. I should add that these thoughts were merely the usual specious arguments one addresses to oneself to maintain optimism at a time when none is justified.

I had saved up a few dollars, enough to pay for the return passage to England and to keep me going while I looked for a job. It was three or four months before I got full-time work—with BBC radio. Those great new opportunities in television had become a series of polite refusals: 'Your name will be kept in mind, but at the moment we need people with experience.' The old familiar problem: how the hell do you get the experience if the only way you can get it is in the job you need the experience for?

When something did turn up at last, in the offer from ITN, I grasped it with both hands and hung on like grim death. I'm afraid that's what a lot of people thought I looked like in my first few weeks as an ITN newscaster.

3. Newscaster

The 'newscaster' system, as described in this account of my early days in ITN, was one of ITN's principal contributions to television journalism. Yet this idea—that the news-presenter should also be a news-reporter with an editorial role in writing and shaping the programmes—has not developed as intended. There has been no British equivalent of Walter Cronkite, the magisterial anchorman of CBS news. Perhaps this is because it is not easy to find good presenters who are also good journalists or vice versa. There is another reason, which has become more important as television's influence has grown, namely the principle that those who actually broadcast should not acquire editorial power especially in news programmes. But if the news-casters of today make only a limited contribution to their news programmes, some of them are much more than announcers and bring to their work their qualities as experienced journalists. Examples in ITN include Sandy Gall and Leonard Parkin; in the BBC Peter Woods and David Holmes (now the BBC's Political Editor).

To the average viewer there may seem no material difference between a news-reader and a news-reporter, between an announcer and a journalist. But to me a newscaster who is also an experienced journalist adds both authority and interest to the presentation of news on television. If television news is expanded and transformed as I have advocated, into a newspaper of the screen, it will be vital that the news-presenters should be experienced journalists, able to link and handle a news-programme which would be much more flexible and wide-ranging than a news-bulletin.

I joined ITN in August 1955. There was only a month to go before transmissions started. The organization was in a state of preparatory chaos on the first and eighth floors of the old Air Ministry building on the corner of Kingsway and Aldwych, now named Television House. The problems of news on television were unknown to most of us. Some of us were from the BBC, some from Fleet Street, some from the cinema newsreels. The recruits from Alexandra Palace knew that Aidan Crawley was aiming at something different from the BBC.

If I had a lot to learn, so had everyone else. Some of the news-room staff were of long experience on newspapers. This did not put me at the disadvantage I had at first feared. Aidan Crawley drummed into our heads that television news required a fresh approach. He ordered everyone to keep an open mind about what they had learnt in Fleet Street, radio, or films, for this might not be applicable to television. I took comfort from the knowledge that Edward R. Murrow, America's most famous television reporter, had never worked on a newspaper. All his journalistic experience had been built up in broadcasting.

I hoped that the various things I had done since leaving the Army would prove useful in learning the techniques of television reporting and, perhaps, in making some contribution of my own.

The most difficult time for me was in the days before transmissions began. ITN's organization was being geared up. The three weeks before the opening night were a hectic shakedown operation. Camera teams were out covering stories, just as if news bulletins were already going on the air. People were asked to give filmed interviews that no one would see, for a news service that did not yet exist. Film was rushed back to ITN to be developed and cut. At scheduled times, for dummy transmission, the film was screened by a portable projector on the bare newsroom wall. The big telecine machines through which film is fed into a TV programme were not yet installed on the eighth floor of Television House.

For these mock news programmes, the producers, newscasters, and sub-editors practised their jobs with the real news as it came in on the tape machines. There were no studio cameras or closed-circuit facilities. The studio was not operational until twenty-four hours before ITN first went on the air. So the mock newscasts had to be done in the news-room with the producer cueing in the film shown on the wall. The newscaster spoke his material to a wooden stand, which was meant to be the camera.

To give some sense of reality. Aidan Crawley assembled the whole of the ITN staff—about 150 people—to be an audience. Editorial and production staff, cameramen, technicians, secretaries, dispatch-riders, office boys—everybody came crowding in to watch those trial news-casts at fixed 'transmission' times. Five minutes before time all these people would pack the newsroom, standing on tables and chairs, waiting for the newscaster to begin. They were a far more unnerving audience than ever the unseen millions were to be. They were curious to see what it was they were all going to be working for—this television news. They usually went away very bewildered and depressed. These newsroom try-outs were invariably a shambles, and bore no noticeable resemblance to a television programme.

The ITN staff audience focused their cold and critical attention on the newscasters. These were the men whom the public would see. These were the men whose personalities and performances might make or mar the combined ITN operation. These were the men whose names and faces would become widely known while the rest of the staff would work anonymously behind the scenes. Were they up to the job, these two, Chris Chataway and—who was the other?—Robin Day? Had they got what it took? I'm afraid the ITN staff were not very impressed. Chris and I hated these mock newscasts and were far worse at them than ever we were when real transmissions began. We both fluffed and fumbled, and morale dropped several points after each dummy run. The staff audience were less hostile to Chris than to me. If they were not sure what sort of figure he would cut as a newscaster, they had all heard of him and realized his celebrity value. But this chap Day—who on earth would switch on to watch *him*, this grim uncongenial bespectacled type? Maybe ITN wasn't looking for glamour boys, but—well—there were limits, weren't there? What on earth had Aidan been up to choosing a chap like Day?

As I waited to begin one of these dummy runs I would look round at the unenthusiastic faces of the secretaries. I knew exactly what they were thinking. I was not their idea of a popular audience-winning TV personality—quite different from the idols built up by the BBC in the early 'fifties: McDonald Hobley, Peter Haigh, Donald Gray. But I also knew that Aidan Crawley was not looking for announcer types. There were to be no announcers in ITN, only newscasters—television journalists who were to acquire their own professional skill and authority. Exactly *why* Aidan Crawley had chosen me, I must admit I did not fully understand. Mine was not to reason why. I knew it was not because of any potentiality as a pin-up boy. All I could do was to ignore the hostility, forget that most of my colleagues couldn't stand the sight of me, throw myself into the job, and hope for the best. It was an uphill fight. Four months passed before I won support from my

ITN colleagues. One particular incident, which I will mention in the next chapter, was the breakthrough to their confidence.

There was an atmosphere of adventure and experiment in Television House. The newscaster system, which ITN was to launch in British broadcasting, was the most adventurous and experimental feature of all. 'Newscasting' was explained by Aidan Crawley at a press conference shortly before the start of ITV. The point seized on by the press was that the newscaster was to 'inject something of his personality'. This idea was received with alarm by many who had grown up to respect the BBC tradition of announcers reading news in the neutral, impersonal style perfected over many years. Crawley's object, however, was not to build up entertainment stars on a par with quiz masters and panellists. Nor was it to launch high-powered controversialists who would twist the news for their own purposes.

'Personality' has become a debased word since the advent of mass television. It is commonly used in at least three ways. It may refer to anyone who has ever appeared on television. (If the appearances have been few and insignificant the description 'well known' is usually added.) It may refer to nonentities who have rocketed to national fame merely through repeated television appearances. It may refer, legitimately, to people whose television appearances reveal personality as in the dictionary definition: 'Distinctive individual characteristics, especially of a marked kind'. Thanks to Gilbert Harding, this use of the word is inevitably reserved in many people's minds for someone who is professionally flamboyant, explosive, or eccentric, and who becomes in time a lovable hate-figure.

If the newscaster was to be merely a well-known nonentity he would contribute nothing. If he tried to ape Gilbert Harding, he would be disastrous. People would either not take the news seriously or would switch off infuriated.

The newscaster system was not a publicity stunt, but hard journalistic common sense. The idea was that as the newscaster became known to viewers, his professional grasp of his material, and his lively interest in it, would make the news more authoritative and entertaining. In that sense only was he to be a 'personality'—a real person, alive to the significance, tragedy, or humour of the news. In that sense, 'personality' should not distract from the news. It should give it added meaning and vitality.

The good newscaster's strength lies not in gimmicks or self-projection, but in straightforward journalistic skill. By that I mean clear, accurate reporting, presented with a personal touch and an individual style. His work should have 'personality' in the sense that a good newspaper article has 'personality'—the distinctive style of an individual person.

The word 'newscaster', introduced to Britain by ITN and flashed on the screen at the end of every ITN bulletin, is now in general use. At first some purists objected to it as a new-fangled bastard Americanism—just how they would expect commercial television to corrupt the English language. 'Newscaster' is admittedly a word imported from the Americans, but it has a respectable pre-television antiquity. For lineage and birth certificate see the *Shorter Oxford English Dictionary*; where the word's earliest known occurrence is given as September 28th 1930:

'*Newscast*: f. NEWS+-cast, of BROADCAST. A wireless broadcast of news. So *Newscaster*, -*casting*.'

Aidan Crawley adopted it for ITN as a contrast to the BBC term news-*reader*, so as to emphasize that a different system had been introduced.

Unlike a BBC news-reader the ITN newscaster was to share in the writing and presentation of the news. He was to be a reporter and not an announcer. He was to take the news items (passed to him by the sub-editors) and put them into a style suited to the spoken word—and, more particularly, to the spoken word as he himself would naturally speak it. The newscaster was to be personally involved in assembling the news. His function was a journalist's function, not that of a human reading-machine or a television equivalent of the printing-press.

This sounded revolutionary in Britain, but had long been accepted practice in American broadcasting. Men like Edward R. Murrow and, more recently, Chet Huntley and David Brinkley have won popularity and respect as journalist-broadcasters in their own right.

Gradually the basic requirements for good newscasting became clear. The newscaster's first job is to understand what he is talking about, to know the background to the items he is handling, so that he can deliver each item with a clear grasp of its significance. He must be *interested* in the news, but not only that, he must *appear* interested. He must get that interest across to people sitting in their homes. He must remember that not all viewers are itching to hear about the talks at Istanbul or the statement by the Sultan of Muscat and Oman. He must not lose heart.

He should try to use good simple English; not journalese, officialese, or slang. The nature of some news items, with verbatim quotations, or phrases required for legal reasons, makes this difficult. Generally, however, there was a lot to be done, especially by avoiding long formal words and by simplifying turgid Government statements. The use of colloquialisms brought one or two protests from viewers who preferred news to be formal and official-sounding. There were a few objections to my use of the word 'bellyaching'. I wrote in reply that no less a person than Field Marshal Viscount Montgomery had made the word respectable. It was good to see that when Mr Carleton Greene became Director-General of the BBC, in 1959, there were signs that those who write BBC news bulletins were being encouraged to use more everyday English. Listening to my transistor in the bath one morning, I was startled to hear the BBC news-reader say that a trade unionist's loss of money stolen at a seaside conference was made up by a 'whip-round' among his fellow delegates. A few years previously that whip-round would have been a collection.

The newscaster must be clear and convincing. To that end, the newscaster must be himself. He must use his own style, his own words (unless quoting), and, when there is some fun in the news, his own sense of humour. That is what Aidan Crawley meant by injecting 'personality'.

These, then, were the essential qualities which a newscaster needed if he was to win public confidence. But the man on the screen had a further task: to win the professional confidence of his colleagues. In television news, as in any television programme which centres on an 'anchor-man', a great deal of the success or failure depends on the newscaster. Dozens of other people make vital contributions; any television programme is a complex team operation. But it is the newscaster who presents the end-product on the screen, and holds it together. Film, of course, is essential, but not all news can be covered by film camera. Cabinet decisions, trials in court, and last-minute news are examples of items which can be reported on TV only by word of mouth. They can be illustrated in various ways, but the events themselves cannot be shown on film. Nor, as yet, can parliamentary debates.

So, however important film may be, the newscaster will always have a key part. If big news breaks just before or during the bulletin it can only be covered by the newscaster. Within a few seconds he must be ready to present it with the right emphasis and to tie it in with the news and film already in the programme. If a 'live' link fails, or if film breaks, the newscaster must cope with the situation as it occurs, filling in as time may require. If he fumbles, or lacks a grasp of his material, or does not look interested in what he is reporting, he spoils the combined effort of the team who have worked to get the programme on the air—the editor who has charge of the whole operation, the news editor who planned the reporting, the cameramen, the producer behind the control panel, the film editors in the cutting rooms, the sub-editors in the newsroom, the engineers, and all the skilled men and women who keep a television news service going. They should all be able to depend on the newscaster not to let them down and not to lose the viewers' interest.

Mere efficiency as a newscaster, difficult enough to achieve, was only part of the battle. The newscaster had also to win approval for his style. In the early days many of my ITN colleagues, doubtless reflecting viewer opinion, had an open dislike of my style. My belligerent interpretation of the newscaster's role in the newsroom had made the sparks fly more than once. The knowledge of his hostility did not make my job on the screen any easier. But I had very clear instructions from Aidan Crawley: a straightforward attacking style, whose keynotes were to be clarity and authority. Several ITN colleagues, with whom I am now the best of friends, have since told me that they pressed Aidan Crawley to get rid of me. I was too unsympathetic, they argued, too harsh in manner. Three things saved me. One was that Crawley was convinced I would get over the difficult stage before long and had the ability to cope with big news in the way he wanted. I was also lucky in the fact that the ITV audience was very small when we started. Everyone was experimenting and only a very small proportion of the total TV audience saw our early efforts. So there was a brief period for us, myself especially, to work ourselves in and to experiment. My other piece of good fortune was that for the first few months of ITN the newscaster upon whom public attention centred was Chris Chataway. He was an instant success as a personality—not merely because fame as a runner had already made him a national figure (his dramatic victory over Vladimir Kuts in the 5,000 metres was fresh in the public mind) but because of his easy, unaffected charm.

Aidan Crawley had taken as big a risk in picking Chris Chataway to be a newscaster as he had in picking me—though in a very different way. In my case the risk was whether my forbidding appearance and fierce approach would ever have any appeal to the mass audiences which commercial television was out to capture. In the case of Chris Chataway the risk was that by choosing a young athletic star (Chris was only twenty-four) as its leading newscaster ITN would be accused of a publicity gimmick and would forfeit any claim to be a serious authoritative news service. Such accusations were muttered by a few sourpusses, but Aidan Crawley's boldness paid off. The determined intelligence that lay behind Chris Chataway's deceptively casual manner soon showed itself in his handling of the newscaster's job. His travels as an athlete to America and Russia had broadened his knowledge.

Six months after ITN began, Chris moved over to BBC *Panorama*. He felt that as a young man whose face was recognized wherever he went his nightly TV appearances were giving him excessive personal publicity in addition to his athletic fame. He wanted to continue on television but less often. He was now keenly interested in politics. As a weekly survey of current issues, *Panorama* was an ideal programme to join.

With Chris Chataway getting all the limelight during ITN's first few months, my own efforts were spared too much attention. I had the chance to dig myself in by the time the ITN network had begun to spread to other parts of the country. But I was still too intense and aggressive for many people's taste. I can only quote Mr Denis Thomas, a television critic, whose account was enjoyed by friends and detractors alike:

'So unequivocal is Mr Day's relish for his job that he seems at times to be daring you to contradict him. He treats the news with an air which I can only describe as proprietorial, as if he had been out and got it all himself. He hunches forward, often into full close-up, narrowing his eyes meaningfully behind glinting spectacles. Or, withdrawing a foot or two, he bites off some item of less than front-page news with an unspoken hint of deeper significance. When a snippet of film shows him conducting an interview, as at Smithfield during the bummaree dispute, he is practically at his man's lapels. In the studio he puts his blunt, loaded questions with the air of a prosecuting counsel at a murder trial. As he swings back to face the cameras, metaphorically blowing on his knuckles, one detects the muffled disturbance as his shaken victim is led away.'

That was the impression recorded by a sophisticated critic. What was the impression on the ordinary viewer? It was no good nursing too many illusions about the impact of high-powered newscasting. Once, during a period of grim and depressing news, a charming middle-aged lady came up to me on the Underground one morning and said: 'Mr Day, I *so* like the way you do your news. You don't look as if you believe a word of it.'

4. Personal Milestone

The importance of the events described in this chapter is much more than the professional significance they had for me at the time. But for the battle fought by Aidan Crawley in 1951, together with the resulting intervention by the Independent Television Authority, ITN might well have ceased to exist as a full-scale service of news on TV. It might even have been reduced to a rip-'n-read service of headline summaries, a minute or so here and there like the weather forecast. That such a danger was even possible seems incredible today when ITN's News at Ten *(running for half an hour and sometimes longer) commands both popularity and respect from its huge audience.*

Aidan Crawley did not continue as editor of ITN for very long. He was involved in a dispute with ITN's Board of Directors. These were the executives from the commercial companies which had jointly established ITN as the network news service. In January 1956 Crawley's resignation was accepted. I had no inside knowledge of the circumstances, but the dispute became a matter of public discussion. There were press comments on the 'sharp differences' between Aidan Crawley and the programme companies. According to *The Times*, the differences were about money, cuts in the news, and ITN's right to expand into background news features. *The Times* commented:

'It would be unfair to imply that Mr Crawley was at issue with all members of the ITN Board, but there are on the board men whose whole experience has been in entertainment and who have scant regard for news as such in a television service.'

There was undoubtedly a feeling in some ITV circles that ITN programmes were too heavy and political, reflecting the approach of its editor and Richard Goold-Adams, his deputy. Goold-Adams also resigned, stating as his reason 'the inadequate role offered to the news company'. In the press the dispute was taken as an alarming indication of the way ITV was going. Those who had been drawn into ITV to organize serious minority features were described as going through 'a harsh winter of discontent'. The losses of the ITV companies were mounting. News appeared to be a suitable field for economy cuts. There were cheaper ways of filling television time than a full news service with world-wide film coverage. It looked a black moment for ITN. The future of the news company appeared in doubt and our jobs in danger.

Although Crawley resigned the editorship he did not lose the battle he had been fighting against cuts in money and air-time. The Independent Television Authority, then under the chairmanship of Sir Kenneth Clark, was emboldened to issue a statement that there was to be at least twenty minutes of news per day. This was the bare minimum required for adequate coverage and economic operation. This ITA ruling was to be the sheet anchor of ITN's existence. Crawley's fight may well have saved ITN from being whittled down to almost complete obliteration. If that was so, why was it necessary for Crawley to persist with his resignation? As the dispute came to a head, the clash between him and the ITN Board took on a personal character. It was whispered by Crawley's critics that he was not content to be a backroom editor but wanted to build himself up as an influential commentator on the screen—a British Ed Murrow. Crawley obviously felt that ITN needed a fresh start under a new editor who was not the object of personal suspicion and who had not been involved in the dispute.

The occasion of Crawley's resignation turned out to be a personal milestone for me. I was newscasting that night. I suggested to Aidan Crawley that we should invite Sir Kenneth Clark, the ITA chairman, to be interviewed in the late bulletin about the ITN dispute and the Authority's role in it. The dispute had been widely reported and there had been severe criticisms of the ITA. Crawley feared that to ventilate the ITN dispute in this way might look like grinding his own axe. Nor, he said, was it possible for him to do the interview himself. As editor, Crawley had been doing some of the important interviews for ITN.

I argued that this was a matter of public importance and that Sir Kenneth Clark should be interviewed just like any other public figure at the centre of an important news story. I offered to do the interview myself. To my surprise, Crawley agreed. To my even greater surprise, Sir Kenneth Clark agreed. I prepared to question him on the late news that night.

I was in a very delicate position. As a member of the ITN staff, I was subject to the editor's control. But the editor and his deputy were personally and publicly involved in this particular news item. I discussed the line of questioning with Aidan Crawley. He tried to persuade me not to put questions which might look as if he was using me for his own purposes. However, with the editor personally implicated as the subject of a major news item, this was a unique situation. The editor was manifestly not the best judge of what questions were to be put. Reminding him of ITN's statutory duty to be accurate and impartial, I told him that I could not skate over anything vital, and would have to use my own judgment.

It was a crucial moment for me and for the staff of ITN. My colleagues—those on duty at TV House and those at home—would be watching anxiously. Aidan Crawley's vision of ITN's future had led many of them to join. Was the news company, for which they had such high hopes, on the brink of extinction? Would a lot of them be sacked? Were they to be denied the chance of building up ITN for effective competition with the BBC News? It is impossible for me to say how far any of these fears were justified—but they existed. Now was the time to clear the air. Sir Kenneth Clark sat unconcernedly beside me in the tiny hot studio waiting for the interview to begin. The *Evening News* TV critic, Kendall McDonald, described the interview as a 'dramatic end to the evening's viewing', and reported:

'Robin Day hammered at Sir Kenneth Clark so hard that at one stage a definitely worried look came into Sir Kenneth's eyes. Full marks.'

I was not consciously 'hammering' Sir Kenneth. I was merely putting simple, straightforward questions to which answers were anxiously awaited.

What, I think, gave the interview its interest was that the chairman of an organization was being publicly cross-examined about his duties by one of the employees. Though this was unusual, if not unique, I had no option but to put questions as in any other news interview. Was Aidan Crawley right to resign? Did Sir Kenneth agree with Crawley that news was not getting its right place? Did he share doubts which had been expressed as to whether companies whose main business was to run light entertainment were the right people to provide news? What was his answer to press criticism of the ITA for being 'weak-kneed' in controlling ITV? The interview continued on these lines for several minutes and overran the bulletin time.

Though Sir Kenneth Clark avoided giving direct answers to some of these questions, the interview drew from him several important declarations of ITA policy. He defended the amount of entertainment on ITV: 'You must capture an audience first of all. When you are established and secure you can gradually build up to a higher level.' But the Authority, he said, had not approved of cuts in the news nor its placing at a later time. 'The Authority believes that a full and responsible news service of at least twenty minutes a day is essential.' From the start, Sir Kenneth declared, the Authority's policy had been that news should be one of the principal items. 'We intend to uphold that.' These answers, obtained from the chairman of the ITA, did something to raise the morale of the ITN staff and to allay their fears for the future.

The interview was a personal milestone for me in several ways. It was my first 'live' television interview. Once on the air, the responsibility was mine, with no repeating or editing possible. Kendall Mc-Donald's report in the *Evening News* was the first favourable press notice I had ever received, after four months of regular TV appearances. Most important of all, the interview won respect from my ITN colleagues. One veteran sub-editor who had clashed sharply with me many times in the newsroom was good enough to greet me the next morning: 'I take off my hat to you.' The questions I had put were the questions which they had been asking and which they never dreamed would be asked on TV. From then on my relations with my ITN colleagues were different. There were no more deputations to the editor to demand my removal from the screen. The reaction was so friendly that I had a sudden feeling of shock at having asked questions which had apparently been so daring. Yet there was nothing outrageous or impertinent, let alone clever, in what I asked. It was simply that they were the questions that needed answering.

It is a significant reflection on what had been the traditional concept of broadcast interviewing that this straightforward interview should have made such an impression. It even impressed a person rarely given to compliments, Michael Peacock of the BBC. He was then beginning to establish a brilliant reputation as the tough young producer of *Panorama*. Shortly after the interview I met him for the first time. 'Your interview with Sir Kenneth Clark,' he said bluntly, 'was the first time you made any real impact on me.' Having since worked for Peacock in *Panorama* and having come to know his exacting standards and reluctance to praise, I now realize that his comment was high tribute.

I do not know how much the ITV chiefs objected to this ventilation of the ITN dispute. I never had any comeback. Nor did Sir Kenneth bear me any ill will. I think he felt that the ITA had improved its reputation by standing up to questions about its responsibilities.

Aidan Crawley was succeeded as ITN's editor by Geoffrey Cox.[1] Crawley had laid down the broad lines of the ITN approach. It was Geoffrey Cox who was to develop these and other ideas over the next few years and build ITN into a national news service. It was fortunate that 'those who had scant regard for news as such in a television service' did not get their way. Soon after Geoffrey Cox became editor, a run of tremendous news burst upon the world: Hungary, Suez, Eden's resignation, Macmillan at Number Ten. ITN resources were strained, but gave these events full and enterprising coverage. The man in the street was following all this news intently. It was just as well for commercial television that its news service had not been mutilated and could rise to a grave international crisis. Otherwise the TAM ratings might have looked pretty humiliating.

For ITN it was not only a period of crisis news. It was the time when commercial television had begun to spread its network throughout the country. First, after London, it opened in Birmingham, then Manchester. The ITV audience was fast increasing. Its share of viewers with sets able to pick up both channels was nearly double that of the BBC. The ITV companies were making heavy losses—but their audience figures were startling. ITV was no longer a service confined to a few hundred thousand London homes. It was becoming a force in the nation's social and political life. The politicians began to watch it carefully. Early on, ITV had not counted much from an audience point of view. Now it mattered. For ITN this meant taking ceaseless care to be politically impartial, without curbing the vigour and spirit of its presentation. It was fortunate that, at this period of crisis news and ITV expansion, ITN should have as its new editor a highly respected journalist with a long background in newspapers, diplomacy, and broadcasting.

[1]Knighted in 1966. Later Chairman of Tyne-Tees Television.

Geoffrey Cox, a New Zealander, had first come to Britain as a Rhodes Scholar. In the 'thirties he was a star reporter on some of the great pre-war stories for the *Daily Express* and the *News Chronicle*. He covered the Spanish Civil War (narrowly escaping execution at the hands of a firing squad), the Anschluss, and the Finnish War. Early in World War II Geoffrey Cox served as New Zealand's *chargé d'affaires* in Washington. He fought with the Eighth Army in Africa and Italy. Since the war he had been with the *News Chronicle*, first as political correspondent and then as assistant editor.

Cox is short and wiry. He has a restrained toughness, typical of many New Zealanders, which can surprise people who do not know him well. He fights his battles shrewdly, choosing the ground and the moment with patience and skill. His dealings with the rival companies which control ITN call for firm diplomacy. He is an expert fly-fisherman. He manages to remain good-humoured and approachable while bearing responsibility for ITN's output seven days a week. He will joke about his cautious preoccupation with keeping a fair balance of views in ITN programmes. One of Geoffrey Cox's favourite stories is about the comment made by one of his staff after the transmission of an ITN *Roving Report* on the Holy Land. It was a reverent, historical programme. 'Any problems?' asked Cox. 'Yes,' said the tired programme editor, 'a call from a chap called Pontius Pilate who said his case had not been properly put.'

To this experienced newspaperman, TV journalism has been an adventure no less than for those who began in it. 'Pioneering this new medium,' says Geoffrey Cox, 'has been as exhilarating an experience as any journalist could wish for.'

For a young man taking up the new profession of television reporting there could not have been two better editors under whom to work than Aidan Crawley and Geoffrey Cox. To Aidan Crawley I owe my original chance. He also gave me the time to improve. To Geoffrey Cox I owe the opportunities of my first big reporting assignments. He gave me full scope to develop the techniques of newscasting, interviewing, and film reporting.

Boldly launched by Aidan Crawley, and now skilfully navigated by Geoffrey Cox, Independent Television News had begun a voyage of discovery into uncharted waters.

5. ITN Sets the Pace

In 1975 it is scarcely possible to believe that the innovations described in this chapter could have been so revolutionary, and so stimulating in their effect on the BBC news. A recent series on BBC 2 called Inside the News *helped to explain why this was so. It included some old recordings of BBC news in the pre-ITN days. I had forgotten how ludicrously ponderous and stuffy they were. Indeed I found myself wondering whether ITN's original impact was not simply due to the fact that almost anything would have been a revolutionary improvement on the old BBC news. But such a reflection is unfair. ITN's achievement was remarkable in itself: that in setting the pace it did not lower the standards.*

The founding of Independent Television News had been a landmark in British journalism. For the first time in many years a new national organ of news had appeared as a daily challenge to Fleet Street and the BBC. Within five months it was built up from scratch into a self-contained organization with its own staff, studios, and equipment, and its own distinctive approach to the news. Just as a newspaper acquires a recognizable personality—through its format, style, selection of news, and familiar features—so does a television news service. The character of ITN, soon established, was in sharp contrast to that of the BBC News. The individual styles of the newscasters were a central feature. Other distinctive ITN characteristics were vivid 'action' film with natural sound, warm human-interest stories, an incisive interviewing style, a robust news-sense, and (revolutionary development!) humour.

ITN newsfilm quickly developed a special character and quality. The aim was to get away from formal, carefully set-up situations as much as possible. None of us gave this approach to filming a name—but we all knew what was wanted. The TV critics called it 'realistic', 'true-to-life'. The use of natural sound was a big element. Sound-recordists went with the cameraman, both often carrying their gear as they walked into rough unpredictable situations. They caught the atmosphere of a strike meeting, a riot, a disaster, in a way that silent film, even with added sound effects, could never do. A silent hand-camera is much more mobile—but the sound camera can bring a scene to life on the television screen. A close-up of an angry striker shaking his fist at the camera, a fanatical schoolgirl screaming 'Eoka' in old Nicosia, Cockney soldiers bargaining with Egyptian street vendors—these need natural synchronized sound to convey the living reality.

ITN reporters, notably George Ffitch and Reginald Bosanquet, would move in with the camera units, interviewing on the spot so quickly that people would forget the camera and microphones, and would speak spontaneously. There was a dramatic interview by ITN at a big open-air strike meeting in Liverpool. Reginald Bosanquet climbed on to the platform to interview Ted Hill, the boilermakers' leader, in front of 3,000 strikers. The interview was accompanied by shouts from the crowd who heard it over the loudspeakers.

One use of this quickfire film reporting became a familiar ITN feature—interviews with the 'man in the street' which are referred to in the BBC as '*vox pop.*' This is now a hackneyed feature of television reporting. Selectively used, however, these 'street' interviews can be television journalism at its best.[1]

ITN's swift and flexible technique in off-the-cuff interviewing got right away from the slow, stiff, staged interview. It caught the warmth and humour of ordinary people in a way that more elaborate filming methods could never do. The man being interviewed on the street corner is not an actor, neither is the reporter. To be their best, that is to say their most natural, they both want the minimum of technical interference and delay, with none of the tension and artificiality that is created by complicated filming operations. ITN made a speciality of using portable 16 mm equipment, of a type which was comparatively new in professional filming when ITN began. Geoffrey Cox, ITN's present editor, states: 'I think ITN can rightly claim to have pioneered the use of the 16 mm camera in many new ways, so as to make it the reporter's note-book in TV journalism.'

These light-weight cameras (the cameraman would prefer me to say '*fairly* light-weight'), and sound apparatus slung round the recordist's neck, could go into action in difficult situations where every second counted. Reporters moved in with the film units to catch the quick comment of an anxious statesman hurrying to his car, an infuriated

[1]See p. 219.

motorist caught in a traffic jam, a bargain-hunting housewife elbowing her way through on the first day of the January sales. These rough-and-ready tactics made heavy demands on the technical skill of the film units. Cameramen were shoved and jostled as they held their cameras in position for longer than seemed humanly possible. Sound-recordists and reporters battled against howling gales and pneumatic drills. Though ITN aimed at top-quality picture and sound, technical purism was not allowed to dominate the filming. Someone's head might get in the cameraman's way at the wrong moment. A crowd might surge, and jolt the sound-recordist as he fought to keep his cables clear and the sound level steady. The reporter's grammar might not be perfect nor his delivery smooth. These were risks inherent in a live, chaotic, crowded situation. They were, indeed, a key element in the realism achieved. A sweating, shivering, shaken reporter and film team would not merely be *covering* the story. They would be *living* the story, and were part of it. You could call it the 'Method' in film reporting.

Some early examples of ITN's realistic film coverage made the critics sit up. The man behind these operations, who nosed out the stories suitable for this treatment, was Arthur Clifford, ITN's brilliant news editor at this time. His job was to plan each day's news assignments. Along with the straightforward coverage of big news, Clifford would send out the reporters and camera teams on dozens of off-beat stories, or on routine stories to be covered in an off-beat way.

There was the occasion when Norman Dodds, MP, caused an outcry by accusing some workmen of laziness. In an experiment which helped to build up the ITN method of realistic reporting, Mr Dodds and the men thrashed it out together with no holds barred. The *Observer* TV critic, Maurice Richardson, commented:

'Five minutes which made any of the organized free speech programmes seem like kissing in the ring. . . . Viewers got a slice of life.'

Bernard Levin wrote in the *Manchester Guardian*:

'Here at last was pure television, television as it ought to be. . . . For five minutes the screen looked in on life and came alive.'

When the Housing Minister went down to the East End of London to launch a slum-clearance drive, ITN strolled with him through the streets. Camera and microphone were there as he knocked on doors and said: 'I'm your Housing Minister. I've come to explain . . .' Millions saw a Cabinet Minister as more than a name or a face. It was not a plug for the Minister. It was fair news reporting—for the viewer also got the reactions of East-Enders, ranging from polite shyness to plain hostility.

Death on the roads was a problem hard to handle in a new way. Handouts, posters, statistics, Commons statements—we had had them all. So before the Whitsun rush ITN interviewed the Minister of Transport out on a main road to the sea as the traffic roared by. ITN confronted the Minister with drivers and cyclists. He appealed to them to take it steady, to come home alive. They squared up to him and demanded something done about better roads. Unconventional television reporting like this brought humanity and humour into the news programmes—but never at the expense of the big political or international issues that dominated the news night after night. ITN's treatment of these issues earned a reputation for boldness and imagination.

A direct and incisive style of interviewing was introduced. This was not a gimmick (though some of its imitators seem to have thought so). It was good journalistic sense. Politicians and public men were asked the questions that needed answering—not 'stooge' questions which the Great Men were graciously disposed to answer. This crisp and concise interviewing was also an elementary necessity for television news. In a TV bulletin of ten or fifteen minutes, an interview can rarely run longer than two or three minutes, generally less.

Editorially, an urgent priority for the infant news company was to establish its own standards of news judgment. There were two reasons for this. The first arose from Section 3(1)c of the Television Act 1954. This laid down that any news should be presented 'with due accuracy and impartiality'.

The BBC News had always followed a similar policy. For ITN, however, it was not enough to carry out its legal duty to be factual and fair. ITN was determined to present the news with humanity, humour, and a spirit of inquiry. Newspapers had been doing this long before anyone had ever heard of ITN. But Fleet Street is free to brighten its pages in ways denied to ITN. The press can speculate, crusade, and attack. ITN could not, because the Television Act said so. ITN was therefore attempting something entirely new in British journalism and broadcasting. It was aiming to combine the punch and sparkle of Fleet Street with the accuracy and impartiality required by Act of Parliament.

The other reason why ITN had to create its own set of news values lay in the nature of television itself. We quickly learned how television affects the selection and arrangement of news. The fact of yesterday's air disaster may no longer be top news tonight—but the *first film* of the scene may well merit first place in this evening's television news. The attempted assassination of Dr Verwoerd at Johannesburg on a Saturday afternoon was an event reported in the utmost detail with photographs in every Sunday newspaper. Yet, when late that same Sunday evening the BBC News received by Comet the ugly and horrifying film of Verwoerd lolling back with blood pouring from his face, this, for television, was news of the highest urgency.

To take another example, a filmed interview may contain no newsworthy statement. It may turn out to be first-class television. The way things are said, the reaction of a face to a question, a revealing pause, the fact that the person may not have been seen publicly for a long time —any of these points may win the interview a place in a television programme. I interviewed Archbishop Makarios in Athens immediately after his release from the Seychelle Islands. Twice I asked him: 'Would you approve of renewed violence in Cyprus if negotiations come to nothing?' No clear statement of policy emerged from the Archbishop's answers. But all the toughness and cunning of the Cypriot leader came across to the viewer. Percy Cudlipp commented in the *Evening Standard*: 'Makarios answered evasively but revealingly.'

When ITN moved into full-scale daily operation principles of news judgment were defined and developed in dozens of situations, each new and different, each demanding special treatment, each teaching a lesson. The robust news sense, which soon became a characteristic of ITN, was seen in the selection and order of news items, and the amount of time given to each one. At this point may I mention the basic difference between news presentation in newspapers and television. A newspaper can spread several big stories and pictures simultaneously on different parts of its front page. A sensational speech may get the main banner headline splashed across the top. A film-star's wedding picture may catch the eye in the middle. An African riot story may be prominently displayed in another part of the same page. All are there for the reader to see at once and to read as he wishes.

A newspaper applies its priorities in the dimension of *space*, television news in the dimension of *time*. In television the importance or interest of an item can be reflected only by the order in which it is seen and heard (first, second, third, etc.) and by the amount of time that is given.

This means that television news is much more limited in the ways in which it can present a combination of important news stories. Sometimes there are two or three equally new and important items. Working in television's time dimension, one of these must come first. Which one? Several factors may decide the question. There may be first-class film to go with one story but not with the others. On television that would make the best 'lead'. Or one of the stories may be closer to the viewers' ordinary life than the others—rail fares up, hire purchase easier—and thus might be most likely to hold their interest and prevent them switching off. On the other hand an item which affects the viewers personally (a rail-fare or hire-purchase story) might be given 'lead' prominence, after a ten-second headline to 'trail' a Khrushchev outburst or some huge take-over bid. This would have acknowledged the importance of that story to the viewers personally and would use this to hold them through the other top stories.

As a general rule, ITN tried to take a middle road between the BBC and the popular press in the order and arrangement of news. Royal items, for instance, were treated on their merits and were not given pride of place automatically. A Ministerial announcement was not to have any special priority. Human stories about unknown people were shown alongside the statements of Authority and the doings of the famous. Crime was to be fully covered, not ghoulishly or morbidly, but as a matter of public concern. If one news item superseded all others in importance ITN would regard itself free to devote the whole bulletin to it. The broad idea was that ITN's coverage should match that of a newspaper's front page. Not having any 'inside pages', ITN would throw everything into a big story on a big night. This was taking a leaf out of the *Daily Mirror*'s book. When the *Mirror* decides the news is really big it doesn't do it by halves. It lays out a huge spread—front, back, and centre—and rubs its readers' noses right in. The impact is tremendous. It has been the same with some of ITN's crisis bulletins. It was not simply the length of time taken, but the robust, energetic handling of the event, that gave these big-night bulletins their strength and sparkle.

One of our special interests was to give the newscasts a lift with something to make the viewer smile. More often than not the film stories—even the 'heavy' ones—would raise a chuckle here and there. The newscaster could add his bit by making the most of some off-beat news item or comic saying of the day. At first we did this only occasionally, without going out of our way, whenever something presented itself. Viewers began to say how much they looked forward to our tail-pieces. Before we knew where we were these had become a regular feature. A mischievous question in Parliament, the matrimonial antics of a film-star, a judge's wisecrack in court—there was something of this sort to be found every day. In spare moments on the news desk I would plough through all the yards of agency tape which had been 'spiked'—that's to say, put aside because it was not needed for the bulletin. Often I would spot some oddity or absurdity that would make a neat ten-second finish to the bulletin—in welcome light relief after the usual catalogue of strikes, bomb outrages, protests, disputes, and so forth. Ot the sub-editors would have spotted something in their reading of the tape. Desmond Grealy, a zany Irishman, who was ITN's chief sub, knew exactly the sort of thing we wanted.

The danger was that once the viewers came to expect a joke at the end—we had to try and produce one. This was the danger signal. Nothing could be worse than dragging in a second-rate joke or footling story. Fortunately we didn't have to rely on the odder news items for a tail-piece. Sometimes no word would be necessary—a shrug of the shoulders or the slightest raising of an eyebrow would make the point without any heavy humour.

The introduction of humour into British news broadcasting—and at times of national crisis too—was a startling innovation. Today it is rather pathetic to remember how daring this appeared at the time. Some comments by Mr Peter Ustinov, writing as guest critic of the *Even.ng Standard* at the time of Mr Macmillan's appointment as Prime Minister, show the impression made by ITN on an independent observer. Ustinov described an ITN bulletin as 'intensely amusing, unpredictable, and alive'. He went on to compare ITN with BBC News:

'I hasten to affirm that I am judging the difference in techniques on a very high level, because the transmission of news is perhaps what television does best, but I still prefer the life and speed of the Independent teams to the calm and dignity of the BBC.'

Then Ustinov recorded one of ITN's classic moments. Its full humour can be appreciated only if you recall the surrounding gravity of the occasion, and the tense political crisis:

'A youthful gentleman in a deer-stalker hat gazing like a pocket Sherlock Holmes at the suspicious door of Number Ten turned out to be unaware of Mr Macmillan's appointment some five hours after its announcement. When told, he said: "Macmillan? Oh, I hope not. They won't like that at Bristol University."'

6. Early Assignments

After hundreds of assignments and programmes during twenty years those which are memorable for me are those which were the first of their kind. The following accounts of four such assignments were written shortly after the events concerned. The visit to Russia with Mr Harold Macmillan in 1959 was my first experience of a major diplomatic mission of this sort, my first visit to Russia, and the first occasion when a visiting television team could attempt anything like normal reporting in Moscow.

The interview in 1959 with Mr Macmillan was the first of its kind with a Prime Minister—that is to say the first of many interviews by myself and others in which Prime Ministers have been questioned at length by a TV interviewer in a way which because it was critical and challenging became a controversial feature of television's contribution to the political process.

The State Opening in 1958 was television's historic first entry into Parliament. It was also my first professional meeting (we were then on opposite sides) with the Master of Ceremonies himself, Richard Dimbleby.

The interview with President Nasser was one of the first world scoops of the new television journalism—not merely because I was the first British reporter to interview Nasser since the Suez invasion but because it was one of the earliest examples of what was called 'telediplomacy' in which world leaders appeared on television to address the people of other countries. Nation spoke unto nation in a new way, though peace was not always spoken.

The interview with Nasser was only six months after Suez. This is how James Cameron reported the interview on the front page of the News Chronicle, under the banner headline 'Colonel Nasser Drops in:

'Sitting in the garden of his Cairo home, President Nasser leaned forward last night into British television screens.

And he asked that we reunite in friendly relations.

He thus did something that had never been done before in the history of international diplomacy.

For the first time on record a national leader submitting a major point of *national policy, by-passed all protocol and sent his message into the homes of another state*—at a time when the two were not in diplomatic relations.

CAIRO, June 1957: It was only seven months since I had driven through the battle-scarred streets of Port Said in a British army jeep, as a reporter with the Anglo-French force. Now I was back in Egypt again, this time for an interview with the man whom Britain and France had tried to crush, an interview with Nasser, in the city that RAF planes had bombed. No British reporter had interviewed the Egyptian President since the Suez crisis. The atmosphere was tense. British citizens had been jailed on spy charges. Britain and Egypt were not in diplomatic relations.

From the Semiramis Hotel, empty but for a few journalists and airline crews, I sent to Nasser's officials the customary indication of main topics (but not the specific questions) which I wished to raise. They warned me against trying to raise some of these topics.

If I did not put these points to Nasser the interview would be a sham. If I did, and he cut short the interview and ordered the confiscation of the film, there would be no interview at all. The editor of ITN had sent me to Cairo only after it had been agreed in negotiations for the interview that I would have complete freedom to question President Nasser. In return, his answers were to be shown in full, subject to any technical difficulty. If there was a last-minute attempt to limit my right to ask questions, I was fully entitled to pull out. On the other hand, I was not to jeopardize the whole operation by making a fuss over an inessential point or by raising delicate issues tactlessly. The responsibility lay on my shoulders. There was no producer. The editor was 2,000 miles away at home with his fingers crossed, waiting for a cable saying 'NASSER INTERVIEW FILMED AS PLANNED'. I decided to speak plainly but politely to Nasser as soon as I was able to get a word with him alone.

The Egyptian President came walking out into the sunshine with one of his little children. I was immediately struck by his size. Gamal Abdul Nasser is a huge man—six foot two, with broad shoulders. He was very friendly. He autographed my copy of his book, *Egypt's Liberation*, the bible of Arab Nationalism. He asked me how much it had cost to buy in England and remarked: 'I don't seem to have made much money from it despite everybody's interest in it.' I strolled with him in his garden, and explained that I felt it essential to raise certain points in the interview. Before I could go into any details he brushed the matter aside and said he didn't mind what I asked. It was a moment of great relief after the long week of waiting in Cairo, a week of wondering when the interview would be fixed, whether it would ever be fixed at all, and whether I would be prevented when the time came, from asking vital questions.

Transcripts of television interviews cannot convey atmosphere or demeanour. The ungrammatical sentences of spontaneous speech, shorn of gesture and emphasis, lose their original impact in a verbatim record. For an impression of how an interview looked and sounded on the screen, one must turn to press descriptions. This is from *Time* magazine's report of the Nasser interview:

'Sitting before the cameras of Britain's Independent Television News—as Russia's Khrushchev did for CBS in the US—Nasser sent an amiable grimace into several million British living rooms. . . . Confronted with a direct question on Egyptian policy toward Israel—whether he really wanted to see its destruction as a state—Nasser tried desperately to fight his way between the Charybdis of a yes that would please Arabs and the Scylla of a no that would mollify the West.

"There is a difference," he said, squirming visibly, "between the rights of Palestine Arabs and the destruction of Israel. We cannot gamble a big war."

"Then," said Day, "is it right that you now accept the permanent existence of Israel as an independent sovereign state?"

"Well, you know," said Nasser, "you are jumping to conclusions."

"No," said Day, "I am asking a question."'

Again Nasser answered. To quote from James Cameron's report in the *News Chronicle*:

'He became lost in the sort of tangled casuistry that passes for fair comment among diplomats, but looks like blotting paper when exposed to common sense.'

None the less, Nasser made one simple point directly to the British people. He had said he was sorry about the period of bad relations and hoped the two countries could be friendly again. It was the twig of an olive branch. Foreign newspapers made much more of this than did our own. It had not sunk in everywhere that Nasser had got his way over

Suez, and that for him to give such a television interview for the country which had invaded Egypt was a remarkable event.

LONDON, February 1958: One Sunday evening I sat in the ITN studio at Television House ready to begin an interview in the weekly series *Tell The People*. On the other side of the table was the Prime Minister. As the cameras were being lined up he derived considerable amusement from the seating arrangement. He complained that whereas he was sitting on a hard upright seat, I was enthroned behind the table in a comfortable swivel chair with well-padded arms. This, said Mr Macmillan, seemed to symbolize the new relationship between politician and TV interviewer. He felt as if he were 'on the mat'. We offered to remove this unintentional impression by changing the hairs, but thePrime Minister, keeping up the banter, said something about knowing his place.

Conservative morale was at rock-bottom after the Rochdale by-election and Mr Selwyn Lloyd, then Foreign Secretary, was under heavy fire from all sides. It was a question about Selwyn Lloyd which aroused the biggest controversy and brought from the PM the most newsworthy answer. The future of Selwyn Lloyd was the number one political talking point. Somehow I had to raise it with the Prime Minister. The editor agreed. How was the question to be put? To ask a Prime Minister if he were going to sack his Foreign Secretary would not get me very far. It might produce a spectacular explosion. It was more likely to be brushed aside as an impertinence. The problem was to phrase a question which would enable the Prime Minister to comment without making him feel he had been asked an insulting question about one of his Cabinet colleagues. The one firm fact I had to go on was that Tory newspapers had been criticizing the Foreign Secretary. This therefore was the basis of the question in the interview:

' "How do you feel, Prime Minister, about criticism which has been made in the last few days, in Conservative newspapers particularly, of Mr Selwyn Lloyd, the Foreign Secretary?" '

The Prime Minister answered calmly and quickly. His reply made banner headlines next morning:

' "Well, I think Mr Selwyn Lloyd is a very good Foreign Secretary and has done his work extremely well. If I didn't think so I would have made a change, but I do not intend to make a change simply as a result of pressure. I don't believe that that is wise. It is not in accordance with my idea of loyalty." '

Later that night I flew to America to interview Vice-President Nixon. At Idlewild Airport next morning I found the Prime Minister's words on the front pages of the New York papers. On returning home a fortnight later I studied the controversy which the interview had aroused in the British press. In the *Daily Telegraph* (one of the Conservative newspapers which had been criticizing the Foreign Secretary) Mr Donald McLachlan asked:

'Should the Prime Minister have been asked what he thought of his own Foreign Secretary, before a camera that showed every flicker of the eyelid? Some say Yes; some say No. Who is to draw the line at which the effort to entertain stops?'

This comment did not quite state the question as it had been put in the interview, but what puzzled me was the suggestion that it had been asked as entertainment rather than as part of a journalist's duty.

The *Manchester Guardian* did not criticize on that score:

'Everybody wants to know what a Prime Minister thinks about his colleagues, and Mr Day asked the right questions: but Mr Macmillan is the first holder of his office to have satisfied public curiosity so bluntly. This may be judged a good or a bad development, according to taste, but it is certainly new. Could one have imagined Sir Winston Churchill when Prime Minister gossiping about Sir Anthony Eden, or Lord Salisbury?'

Was 'gossip' the word to describe Mr Macmillan's reply?

The *Observer* seized on the fact that the Prime Minister had been interviewed on TV but not by the press. Constitutional history had been made; it declared, and Mr Macmillian may not have realized what a revolutionary thing he was doing. The *Observer* went on:

'There is a good case for saying that the public has a right to see and hear its leaders expound their policies in this direct and effective way.

But if the Prime Minister can be interviewed on TV, why should he
not be interviewed by the press which is a much more subtle instrument
for conveying—or concealing—his thoughts?'

I am not sure that I understand the point of a press conference which
conceals a Prime Minister's thoughts. Concerning the rights of the press,
it is well known that from time to time newspapermen have the op-
po rtunityof private talks with Prime Ministers and other Cabinet
members. These off-the-record occasions can be much more useful than
a public press conference. The television camera can make no use of
such occasions. One sphere in which the press need not fear the rivalry
of television is in the interpretation of events behind the scenes, and
the analysis of invisible factors.

It was Cassandra (Bill Connor of the *Daily Mirror*) who lashed out
most fiercely about my Selwyn Lloyd question:

'If anybody wants a demonstration of the power of television let him
refer to the interview which Mr Robin Day had with the Prime
Minister on ITV on Sunday night.

Mr Day, who is a formidable interrogator, suddenly asked Mr
Macmillan how he felt about criticism in Conservative newspapers
"particularly of Mr Selwyn Lloyd".

At once the Queen's First Minister was put on the spot.

What *else* could he say about his colleague?

How *could* he suddenly reject him?

How *could* Mr Macmillan be anything but complimentary to his
colleague—and to his accomplice in the Suez escapade?

So here you have the ridiculous situation of how the British Prime
Minister can suddenly be put on a Morton's Fork which forces him into
defending and maintaining a colleague who is obviously a disaster to
British foreign policy.

Mr Robin Day by his skill as an examiner has been responsible for
prolonging in office a man who probably doesn't want the job and is
demonstrably incapable of doing it.

The Idiot's Lantern is getting too big for its ugly gleam.'

Cassandra may have been right about the Idiot's Lantern, but he was
wrong about the Morton's Fork. The Prime Minister was *not* put on the

spot. As it happens, I know that Mr Macmillan expected a question about his Foreign Secretary. This was not through any prior notice from me or anyone in ITN. There had been only the broadest outline of topics—the H-bomb, the Government's political problems, etc. But the fact is that the Prime Minister was ready for a question about Mr Selwyn Lloyd and was fully prepared to defend him. Those like Cassandra, who feel that Mr Selwyn Lloyd should have left the Foreign Office much sooner than he did, must therefore blame the Prime Minister and not me.

At the time of this interview, Mr Macmillan's political talents had not become apparent to the mass of the voters. 'Supermac' had not yet appeared on Vicky's drawing-board.

The Prime Minister had appeared on BBC *Press Conference* earlier that week, but had not been stimulated by his questioners, whom *The Times* described as 'a restrained group'. Three days later, in the ITN interview, he made a tremendous personal impact, defending his Foreign Secretary and delighting his supporters. In the *Daily Express* Derek Marks described Mr Macmillan as

'firm and confident in the face of vigorous questioning . . . certainly the most vigorous cross-examination a Prime Minister has been subjected to in public.'

The *Daily Telegraph* noted:

'The Prime Minister's replies were more direct and quicker to the point than in his BBC interview.'

The *Yorkshire Post*:

'Tories will be delighted with the Prime Minister's television success. Certainly he is no longer just a House of Commons man.'

It is not the business of a television interviewer to try to help or hinder any politician's television popularity. His job is to ask questions. If the Prime Minister came out well, as he did, that was because he could respond in masterly fashion to straightforward questioning. Pendennis of the *Observer* reported that the Prime Minister 'did not at all resent his tough (and quite impromptu) questioning from Robin Day'.

I later heard that Mr Macmillan himself had referred to this interview as the first time he had really mastered television. At all events the Prime Minister had made his breakthrough as a television figure. When, shortly afterwards, he did a leisurely half-hour's interview for CBS Television, with those distinguished questioners Edward R. Murrow and Charles Collingwood, Mr Macmillan was able to display his television talent with impressive effect.

RUSSIA, February 1959: A sumptuous dinner of caviare, chicken à la Kiev, and champagne had been served. In the dining-car of the Red Arrow express journalists from all over the world had settled down to a party.

They were tired but happy men—tired after trudging through the snow and slush of Leningrad after Mr Macmillan, and happy because for the first time on the Prime Minister's Russian trip they were free from cables and telephones, beyond the reach of their offices. Mr Drew Middleton, the distinguished chief of the *New York Times* London Bureau, was singing 'Home on the Range' in approximate harmony with Mr Don Cook of the *New York Herald Tribune*. Mr Malcolm Muggeridge was arguing heatedly with Mr Charles Curran. Mr Don Iddon and I were toasting in Russian champagne the merits of caviare, chicken à la Kiev, and Russian champagne.

It was the most opulent train journey any of us had ever known. De-luxe coaches of Tsarist grandeur had been added to the Red Arrow, making its nightly run along the dead-straight railroad from Leningrad to Moscow. Our sleeping-cars were even more magnificent than the dining-car. They had velvet furnishings, plush carpets, elegant tables, reading-lamps, and private shower-baths.

On this luxurious train we were nearing the end of Mr Macmillan's 'voyage of discovery'. Surprise had followed surprise from Macmillan's hat to Khrushchev's toothache. The world watched as the Russians practised their Pavlovian psychology, with the British Prime Minister as the dog to be baited and demoralized.

With ITN cameraman George Richardson and recordist Mick Doyle I followed the Prime Minister during those fantastic ten days. Snubbed by Khrushchev, Macmillan went to Kiev and plodded on with the tour escorted by minor Russian officials. He looked utterly worn out as we filmed him inspecting the Museum of Ukrainian National Economy. The camera caught the Prime Minister's expressionless face as he listened to the Russian translator's interminable recitation of figures showing the increase in sugar-beet production since 1925. Around the Prime Minister were the reporters, familiar faces under unfamiliar fur hats. Moss Bros must have made a fortune. Not only the journalists, but Mr Macmillan's entourage of officials, secretaries, and security men had hired fur-lined boots, heavy astrakhan coats, and fur hats. The Prime Minister alone appeared to be wearing something out of his own wardrobe, that magnificent white sheepskin hat, inches taller than the Russian fashion. This was the picture of the year.

There were over a hundred journalists with the Prime Minister's party. So often a TV reporter tends to work alone with his camera crew. On this Russian trip the company was almost as fascinating as the assignment itself.

Malcolm Muggeridge, with his eloquent cigarette-holder, was representing the *Daily Mirror*. He thought the whole trip was a farce. In tones of supreme contempt Muggeridge would describe Macmillan as a month-eaten Galsworthian figure labouring under the delusion that he could deal with the ruthless gang in the Kremlin. Emrys Hughes, MP, was reporting for *Tribune*. He was very pleased with both Macmillan and Khrushchev. He derived huge amusement from the eulogy which the Prime Minister had lavished on Khrushchev in the Russian tradition of after-banquet speaking:

'This is a truly constructive life's work which you have undertaken. The future before the Soviet people is one of expanding horizons. Across the steppes glows the furnace of industry beckoning to a promised land. This is no mirage which you see before you. It is sober reality. The rate and quality of your progress are indeed extraordinary and—so far as I know—unparalleled in history.'

Cyril Ray, of the *Spectator*, a *bon vivant* in Russia no less than elsewhere, would advise on food and wine. David Floyd, the *Daily Telegraph*'s learned expert on Russian affairs, would translate menus and newspapers for us. The imperturbable Harold Evans, the PM's public-relations man, did his tightrope job of helping news-hungry journalists as much as he could without giving anything away. Randolph Churchill stung his colleagues by securing an interview for the *Evening Standard* with Guy Burgess, heckled the Foreign Office spokesman mercilessly, and stormed at Intourist about his hotel accommodation. Randolph did not stay the whole trip. He left us at Kiev and went to Bournemouth, where he was interested in a by-election. The rest of us flew with the Prime Minister to Leningrad. At the airport there we found the Russians had decided it was time to give the dog another bone. Our cameras filmed the surprise appearance of Deputy-Premier Mikoyan, with peace and co-operation all over his smiling face. Macmillan's speech was courteous but his face betrayed no sense of relief. The dog was not biting that easily.

For a television reporter this Russian trip had marvellous oppor-tunities and almost insuperable difficulties. Film censorship had been lifted for the trip. We had a unique chance to film and interview. Almost anything we filmed would be of interest. Time was the snag. All Macmillan's public movements had to be covered for the news bulletins. Only when he was closeted in talks with the Russians could we look for feature material. In those ten hectic days we filmed over twenty items for the ITN bulletins and, on top of that, two half-hour features for *Roving Report*. Only on the evening before Mr Macmillan's arrival was there time to have a night out. Several of us went to one of Moscow's best dining-spots. It was the equivalent of a good Soho restaurant. The food was excellent, the price was high. Apart from the slow service, there was one striking difference. Several of the guests were blind drunk. One of them got very nasty when I objected to him pouring his wine into my coffee. The Russians at the table next to ours were standing, swaying, and shouting. It appeared to be quite normal. Nobody seemed to mind.

The first time we dispatched film from Moscow we came up against the blank obstructiveness which stems from the habit of unquestioning obedience to authority, and which is a feature of life under Communist bureaucracy. We had arrived in Moscow two days before Macmillan to film some scene-setters. When we tried to ship this film our official interpreter informed us this was impossible. She said that the censorship would not be lifted until Macmillan's visit began. This was ridiculous.

'Who said so?' I inquired.

'The official responsible,' she said.

I swore, hoping her English did not extend that far.

'Where is he?' I asked.

'You cannot see him.'

'Why not?'

'He is busy.'

'Would you please take me to him?'

'It would do no good.'

'How do you know?'

'He said the regulation is quite clear.'

'How can I get an exception made?'

'It is not possible.'

'But who *could* give me permission?'

'The Foreign Ministry in Moscow.'

'Could you ask them for me?'

'No, I could not. I am only an interpreter.'

'Well, who at the airport could help me?'

'No one except the Commandant of Air Transport.'

'Where is he?'

'I do not know.'

'Would you find out?'

With the utmost reluctance, our interpreter, a dumpy, sour-faced young woman, went to make inquiries. She returned looking a bit more pleased.

'The Commandant of Air Transport is busy.'

'Where is his office?'

'You cannot go there.'

'Why not?'

'It is not allowed.'

'Why can't we go there and see?'

'It will do no good.'

'But whether he can see me or not, I would like to know where his office is.'

The Commandant's office was very close by, just up the stairs. Up we went.

'Would you please ask if I could see him for a moment?'

She went in sullenly, and emerged a moment or two later.

'He is busy.'

'How long will he be busy?'

'I do not know.'

'Would you please ask?'

Slowly she was being worn down. I was getting a perverse enjoy-ment out of this piece of brain-washing in reverse, this indoctrination in the evil democratic principle of not taking no for an answer.

'The Commandant has someone with him; we must go back to Moscow, it is late.'

'We will do nothing of the sort. It is only four o'clock. We will wait till the Commandant is free.'

Our interpreter was furious. I think that she was beginning to sense defeat. She sat in silence with us on the hard wooden benches outside the Commandant's door, while the cameraman and I kept each other's spirits up. After an hour and a half I felt that the Commandant had given more than adequate time to his caller.

'Would you inquire again, please?'

By this time our interpreter was breaking—she made no protest. But I went in with her. There was the Commandant—alone—a charming fellow in a smart blue uniform. What could he do for us? Our mission was explained. I held up the small envelope of film. Could it please go on the Scandinavian Airlines flight at nine o'clock? The peace-loving people of Britain, I said, were eagerly awaiting pictures of the places which were to be the scene of these historic talks in search of friendship and co-operation. I was beginning to sound like a *Pravda* editorial. The Commandant was all smiles. He picked up the phone, talked to someone for about two minutes. I could see it was going to be all right. He put the phone down.

'Certainly—I will see to it myself. There is no difficulty.'

Never have I had such a glorious sense of victory. The film went as planned and was on the screen the next night. Our interpreter never forgave me. After two or three similar experiences, she gave up and asked to work with someone else.

While not everyone had such an awkward interpreter, we all found that in Moscow our relationship with these ladies was somewhat cold. 'Will you join us for coffee?' 'No,' they would say, and would wait outside till we were finished. In Kiev and Leningrad they were not quite so formal. In Kiev they danced rock-'n'-roll with us. My attrac-tive young interpreter in Leningrad, like all her generation avid for Western jazz, turned to me in our car and said: 'Mr Day, would you do me a favour? Would you tell me the words of "I Can't Give You

Anything But Love, Baby"?' Fortunately for the cause of Anglo-Soviet friendship I was able to oblige.

With our sound-film unit we filmed as much as we could of Russian life as the trip proceeded. In Leningrad it happened to be 'election' day. Outside a polling booth I interviewed the Returning Officer. I'm afraid we never began to get on the same wavelength. The idea of free elections which lay behind my questions had no meaning to this Russian working man—nor indeed to the interpreter, who began to query my questions. The vast gulf between the two systems was never more apparent. Yet one saw that these Russians knew no other meaning of the word democracy and were proud of their system. In that sense alone they were democratically governed.

A more delicate interview took place with a young English-speaking graduate of Moscow University. He was highly intelligent. He had not confined his study of English literature to Charles Dickens. He had read Evelyn Waugh, Graham Greene, and John Osborne. I wanted to know if he, unlike the less-educated Returning Officer in Leningrad, had any understanding of our kind of democracy. After his orthodox description of the 'democratic' Soviet constitution I asked him if it would not be a good idea if there were as open criticism in Russia of Khrushchev as there was of Macmillan in Britain. Before he could answer there was a camera hitch, which took a few moments to correct. 'I must go,' said the young man. 'I am late.' A crowd had begun to gather in the gardens of Sverdlov Square where we were filming. It had been with only the greatest difficulty that I had persuaded him to be interviewed. He was very jumpy. At that moment the camera was ready and before he could get up from the bench I put the question again.

' "No," he said. "There is no need for criticism of Mr Khrushchev."
   "Why not?"
   "Because Mr Khrushchev has the support of all the Russian people." '

He half rose from the bench to leave. Quickly I shot a final question:

' "But don't you think it would have been better in Stalin's lifetime if there had been a system which allowed criticism?" '

Our eyes met, and, I think, our minds also. He knew what I was getting at. He paused for a long time—I should say about ten to fifteen seconds. It seemed as if he was wondering whether I really expected an answer. Pushing the microphone closer to him, I made it clear that I did. At last his answer came in a whisper:

' "I guess it would!" '

The silent seconds before he replied had spoken for the mental torment in the mind of this young Russian intellectual. He jumped up from the bench and almost ran from Sverdlov Square. The watching crowd must have wondered what had happened.

At the Prime Minister's press conference there was an incident in which I was involved. I did not come very well out of it. The press conference was a joint affair for newspapers and television. I expected to be able to get in one question for ITN. I telephoned London for advice. What was the main talking point at the conclusion of the Prime Minister's visit? I was given two suggestions: the prospect for Summit talks, and the timing of the General Election which speculation had fixed for May or October 1959. Questions were put about Summit prospects long before I could catch the Prime Minister's eye. So, when my turn came, I put a question about the likely date of the British General Election. In the effort to be brief, the point of the question did not get across clearly. This was whether an election was likely before the autumn in view of the pre-Summit negotiations during the spring and summer. Unfortunately Mr Macmillan must have taken the question as implying that his Moscow visit had been undertaken for electioneering purposes. Nothing was further from my mind. Like most people in Britain, I fully supported the Prime Minister's efforts. Even if I hadn't, it would not have been my business to show it. Anyway, Mr Macmillan put that interpretation on my question. He delivered a crushing rebuke in front of 300 reporters. 'That is a question,' he said, 'from the wrong man in the wrong place.' I was well and truly slapped down. Afterwards my newspaper colleagues twitted me mercilessly. The Prime Minister's public rebuke of one of their bumptious television rivals had delighted them. On no other occasion have I known such back-slapping *bonhomie* from newspapermen. Mr Macmillan's remark had stung me for the moment, but if an interviewer's question misfires he must take the consequences, especially on this occasion when the

Prime Minister was in no mood to banter. As Cyril Ray commented
in his account of this incident in the *Spectator*:

'In the flash of asperity at the Hall of Journalists one could guess what
it must be like to be subjected to alternate slaps on the wrist and pats
on the back; three ceremonial visits to the ballet in three widely
separated cities in four days . . . when all you really want to do is to
curl up with your bullet-holed copy of Æschylus.'

My worry was that the incident would embarrass the editor of ITN,
but I asked that it be shown on the screen, however foolish it made me
look, and it was.

WESTMINSTER, October 1958: At half past nine in the morning I
climbed up through a trap-door into a wooden cubicle the size of a
telephone kiosk. It had been installed high up between the Victorian
Gothic arches of the House of Lords Chamber. The small glass window
looked across to the golden throne at the other end. It was a historic
day for both Parliament and television. The State Opening of Parliament by Her Majesty the Queen, a ceremony second only in splendour
and solemnity to the Coronation, was to be televised for the first time.
A few feet away, in a companion cubicle, Richard Dimbleby had
squeezed into his position. He was to provide the commentary for
BBC viewers; I was the ITV commentator. 'Dimbleby *v.* Day' was the
theme of press comments, or, as the *Daily Express* put it, 'The Gentleman versus the Chap'.

This was an assignment in which practically everything was against
me. As the ITV commentator I was a novice competing with the
master craftsman, a man who knew from countless royal occasions
every jewel in the Imperial Crown and every stitch on a herald's tabard.
The TV pictures were being provided by the BBC and 'fed' to ITV.
This put me in the awkward position of having to comment on a
sequence of pictures selected by a producer who was following
Dimbleby's words. Supposing, for instance, that Peter Dimmock, the
BBC producer, had shown a shot of King George V's statue and was
about to go to a shot of the Victoria Tower. Dimbleby would be saying '. . . *and there is the memorial to the Queen's grandfather the beloved
Sailor King* . . .' Dimmock, whose camera instructions were heard on
headphones by Dimbleby and myself, would shout '*coming to Victoria*

Tower'. At this, Dimbleby would skilfully wind up his remarks about King George V and lead into a shot of the Victoria Tower, like this: '*. . . the beloved Sailor King, George V, whose statue stands across the road opposite the great Victoria Tower'*. Meanwhile I would be trying to do the same thing. The difficulty was that though Richard Dimbleby was, like myself, following Peter Dimmock's cues, the exact moment at which Dimmock put a given picture on the screen would be time to fit Dimbleby's words. As soon as Dimbleby got to the word '*Victoria*', up would come the tower on the screen. The BBC had provided me with details of the order and timing of shots to be taken by their cameras. Even so, it was pure luck whether my words fitted the pictures as closely as Dimbleby's. It was an exceedingly tricky business to form appropriate phrases with the roar of the crowds and bands in one ear, and Dimmock shouting his control-room instructions in the other: '*Coming to Horse Guards Arch—where are you, Camera Seven? . . . Coming to Horse Guards Arch now. . . .   Hurry up, Richard. . . .*'

Another problem facing me was that of style. Only the BBC had been allowed to install cameras, but the ITV network had been given the right to have their own commentator. It was made clear to me that something different from the traditional BBC style, exemplified and embodied by Richard Dimbleby, was required. It was not made clear how this difference was to be achieved. This was left entirely to me. How *could* one be very different in tone from Dimbleby when describing a solemn royal occasion? Yet any attempt to imitate or out-do the master with majestic, flowing descriptions was doomed to failure. The problem baffled me for some time. Then I realized I was approaching it in entirely the wrong way. There was no need for me consciously to aim at a different style from Dimbleby, for we were different people with different approaches to the occasion. My simple objective should be to look at the ceremony in my own way and the style would naturally follow.

There was one main theme in my approach throughout the several weeks' preparation for the broadcast: that this was not just another ancient royal ceremony—it was a profoundly significant expression of modern political realities. Descriptions of ceremonial details were obviously necessary to assist the viewer, but I tried to give these without adding to any unnecessary verbiage. As far as possible I tried to let the splendour of the ceremony speak for itself. My principle function was to convey its contemporary meaning. This was a theme to which I returned again and again. For instance, as the cameras showed the magnificent scene of the lords assembled around the throne:

'This morning's ceremony ... dramatizes the working principles of our parliamentary system: who has the pageantry and who has the power—principles won in the struggles of the past.'

Over a shot of the throne:

'. . . though the Throne is still the seat of Majesty, it is no longer the seat of power.'

As the cameras surveyed the ornate chamber crowded with peers and peeresses:

'. . . the story of the British Parliament is simply the story of how power has been taken away from the Throne, which you saw, and from this room—taken to the other room down the corridor, through that archway in the centre, from which the House of Commons will come.'

Again, as the glittering assembly awaited the Sovereign's arrival:

'That's how we have done it in Britain. The Monarch has the pomp without the power, the Commons have the power and no pomp. The Lords, as you see, have their pomp, but very little power.'

This approach gave some people the impression that I was trying to belittle the ceremony, which was not true. I was conscious of the fact that this ancient ceremony was being seen for the first time by a vast audience far outside the privileged few who had attended it in the past. My aim was to put the traditional pageantry into modern perspective. At preliminary discussions of the television arrangements, I mentioned to the Queen's Private Secretary, Sir Michael Adeane, that I thought this theme should be stressed in the commentary. He not only agreed but drew my attention to a point which would help me. 'Notice,' he said, 'that the Queen, though she is the Sovereign, must wait for the Commons, the people's representatives, to arrive. Under a less democratic type of monarchy it would be the other way round.'

The passages which caused particular irritation were at the very end of the commentary. These were thought by some to be much too down-to-earth and brusque at a moment which called for a purple peroration—the moment when Her Majesty left the chamber:

'A new session of Parliament has been opened. The Queen will go back to Buckingham Palace. The crown will go back to the Tower of London. All the scarlet and ermine robes will go back to wherever they came from. And Parliament will go back to work; to pensions, education, unemployment, strikes, Cyprus, disarmament, and the rest of it. The few moments of pageantry in the working life of Parliament are over.'

Finally, as the cameras cut to an end-shot of the empty throne:

'Everyone is wondering at Westminster what Government will write the next speech from this throne. Before Her Majesty sits on it again there may be a General Election. That is when we have our say. And what Her Majesty reads from this throne depends on what we put in the ballot box.'

It may be added that this concern with the political realities behind the ceremony was also emphasized, in more formal language, in the Speech from the Throne. Referring to the millions who were watching on television, Her Majesty concluded:

' "Outwardly they will see the pageantry and the symbols of authority and power, but in their hearts they will surely respond to the hope and purpose which inspire our parliamentary tradition." '

I was determined not to let either the pageantry or its political significance make the commentary too solemn. This was not a funeral or any kind of religious ceremony. There was no reason why a little humour, provided it came naturally, should not be introduced. This was striking a new note. It was risky. I plucked up more courage when, much to my surprise, the Earl Marshal and Garter King of Arms laughed uproariously at one or two mildly humorous touches which were slipped into the commentary for the recorded rehearsal.

On the day itself, several such remarks were included. They were all very gentle and the commentary was ninety-five per cent serious, but they were picked up in the press as a sharp break with broadcasting tradition. Over a shot of Monty who had recently been making headlines with provocative speeches:

'. . . Field Marshal Montgomery, who has a silent role on this occasion.'

As the Great Officers of State preceded the Queen towards the Royal Gallery:

'. . . the Lord Great Chamberlain and the Earl Marshal walking up the stairs backwards. That must be very tricky, but they are both very experienced at these operations.'

A little harmless irony over the Beefeaters' symbolic inspection of the vaults:

'Now that we know that such an obviously thorough search has been carried out and that Parliament will not be blown up . . .'

A remark which some thought decidedly lacking in taste was the reference to the scarlet and ermine robes going back 'to where they came from'. I had at least refrained from quoting the Duke of Windsor's account of a State Opening. He tells us in *A King's Story* that as he looked at the brilliant scene his senses were assaulted by an almost suffocating smell of mothballs.

In general, the occasional touches of humour were welcomed by the press, though one newspaper rapped me sharply over the knuckles. No, not *The Times*, which referred to 'a few agreeably dry asides', but the *Daily Express*! Its TV critic James Thomas, sternly admonished: 'This kind of function is no place to display even a quiet wit.'

The occasion was a triumph for the BBC Outside Broadcast unit. For me personally it went off better than I had dared to hope. The ITV audience was generally less than the BBC's, but it held up very well considering Dimbleby's great reputation for these things, and the fact that BBC pictures were being used. It was also ITV's first share in a big ceremonial occasion. Viewers who wrote to me were mostly in favour of my commentary style—but an infuriated minority were not. One gentleman undoubtedly expressed the feelings of many:

'The broadcast of this memorable occasion was ruined on the ITV. Robin Day was hopeless. Please never again (repeat never) let the multitudes have to listen to him on occasions of this kind. Luckily for myself I was able to listen to the rich tones of Richard Dimbleby who commented with dignity and culture.'

I had made a life-long enemy of a lady in Buckhurst Hill, whose name, believe it nor not, was Mrs Grundy:

'I was appalled and disgusted by the commentary given by Mr Robin Day—he was cynical, contemptuous and treated it all as a big joke. It was a wonderful ceremony and worthy of a better and more patriotic commentator.'

7. The TV Interview: Thoughts and Reflections

The interview has now been long established as a basic instrument of TV journalism and as a controversial talking-point for viewers. But twenty years ago this branch of the new journalism was in its infancy. The passages which follow were written during that early period when the techniques and principles of TV interviewing were being hammered out by experience. I have included some thoughts which are not irrelevant today and some recollections which have personal significance for me.

THE GROOMING NONSENSE

Most public men neither need nor desire cotton-wool treatment. As British politicians have got used to television, the ablest of them have found that a vigorous, penetrating interview brings out the best in them. It stimulates them to be more forceful and convincing. For some, of course, the result is quite different—they appear pompous, evasive, and insincere. This is not the fault of television or the interviewer. That type of politician is pompous, evasive, and insincere at any time—at a meeting, or in Parliament. If someone who is being interviewed has a good case to argue and gives straightforward answers he has nothing to fear. Public sympathy will be on his side if the interviewer tries to be clever or aggressive.

The big political parties have spent huge amounts of money on special TV studios for 'grooming' their politicians. There is a frightful lot of rubbish talked about this. A politician may need *practice* on TV, but that can only be acquired in real programmes. This is the ordinary business of gaining confidence, no different from gaining confidence in speaking on a platform. You cannot 'groom' people into giving effective answers in a TV interview, any more than you can 'groom' them into being persuasive platform orators. There is no special magic about television. It is an instrument of communication, which shows what it sees. If what it sees is uninteresting, that is that. An inexperienced person who makes mistakes and appears nervous on TV may well have a greater personal impact than a smooth dimwit who has graduated from a TV charm school. No politician needs TV coaching who has the qualities which command respect in Parliament or any company: sincerity, clarity, and brains. If he lacks these no amount of coaching will make him effective on TV. It is quite possible that he may do brilliantly on TV without possessing any of these qualities. That is quite a different matter, attributable to some compelling quality of personality, some strange individual magnetism, but such gifts are beyond the creative power of television 'advisers'.

What advice can be given to politicians who lack TV experience? This question was put to me and a producer colleague by an official who gave TV 'training' to the duller members of one of the big parties. We gave the hackneyed but absolutely true answer: 'Be themselves.' 'That,' the official replied, 'is what I am afraid of.'

MR FUJIYAMA AND THE BALL-BEARINGS

A familiar complaint about television interviewers is rudeness. Where should the line be drawn? There is no point in asking a question for the sake of being offensive. Rudeness merely obscures the issue. But the interviewer should not be deterred from putting a vital question merely because it might cause offence. Politicians, in particular, can be very sensitive; so can their more bigoted supporters. They must take the rough with the smooth. The distinction between rudeness and plain speaking is very narrow. It is a question of opinion. The viewer must be left to judge.

I was accused of gross discourtesy in an interview with the Japanese Foreign Minister, Mr Fujiyama, who visited London in 1957. The extraordinary scene at the Dorchester Hotel, in full view of newspaper reporters and photographers, was none of my making. I had with me a Japanese ball-bearing packet and the original British article of which it was a copy. Pirating of British designs had been in the news as a matter of extreme annoyance to British businessmen. Newspaper reporters raised it at the press conference which Mr Fujiyama gave immediately before my filmed interview. It seemed only sensible for a TV reporter to produce visual evidence of these practices. I had no thought of creating a rumpus. When I produced the two ball-bearing packets and asked what the Japanese Government was going to do about it, the Japanese interpreter was furious.

'This is out of order,' he snapped. 'If you had this in mind you should have given the Minister advance notice.'

This was a silly piece of official small-mindedness. The Minister had readily answered questions on this subject at his press conference. He would have been quite capable of doing so in the TV interview if the interpreter hadn't butted in. I replied: 'The Minister did not ask for advance notice of questions.' With the ITN camera still turning, poor Mr Fujiyama sat puzzled and silent between us. The Japanese interpreter exploded: 'This is treachery.' I could scarcely believe my ears. Keeping as much control of myself as possible, I held up the ball-bearing packets for the interpreter and the camera to see and retorted: 'But British manufacturers regard *this* as treachery.' (I realized how mild-mannered this retort had been when I met Mr Aneurin Bevan a few days later. Nye had seen the interview: 'You should have said "Pearl Harbor to you, boy, Pearl Harbor to you." ') After two or three minutes another Japanese official realized the whole business was being recorded on film and marched in to stop everything.

The incident had repercussions. It upset the British Foreign Office. A former British Ambassador to Tokio wrote to the press accusing me of gross discourtesy to a visiting statesman. In Japan a newspaper columnist wrote that Mr Fujiyama had been 'treated spitefully', but he added:

'The British have something to complain about. It is shameful to report that Japanese manufacturers have been pirating British designs. Our manufacturers should use their original talents ... otherwise our Ministers will be subjected to stronger criticism when they visit overseas capitals.'

There were other consequences of this 'discourteous' interview. A week later Mr John King, managing director of Pollard Bearings Ltd, received a letter from Singapore informing him that Bollard Bearings (the Japanese version of Pollard) were to be withdrawn in that area.

TECHNIQUES AND TACTICS

Interviews may be divided into two kinds: those in the studio (which may be 'live' or recorded) and those filmed on location (at home or overseas). In the studio the main point is that each operation is a once-for-all affair. There is no repetition, no editing. Timing must be exact. (Even when a studio interview is tape-recorded for later transmission the aim is to do it exactly as if it were 'live'.) On the other hand, a studio interview has many advantages over filming. It is a 'live' performance with the feeling of a vast audience watching. Reactions are heightened by the sense of occasion. Mental processes are at their pitch of concentration. The performance is usually fresher, warmer, more spontaneous than it would be on film.

Filming is unavoidable on many occasions. There are still a vast number of situations in which a 'live' interview is either impossible or undesirable. Even in foreign countries with which there is a direct TV link, 'live' TV cameras cannot go to every place or person you want and it is no good doing everything in a studio. A studio in Paris looks remarkably like a studio in Lime Grove or anywhere else. Film units of the 16 mm type are by far the most flexible and convenient way of reporting for TV. They carry their own batteries and are completely self-contained. They can go into action anywhere at a few minutes' notice. Another great advantage of film is that you can shoot more than you need. You have a greater choice of material. If you are not satisfied you can have a second go—though not always. A riot incident or an assassination cannot be repeated for the convenience of a TV film unit. An angry or humorous remark can only be truly caught the first time it is said.

There are some basic points of technique that apply to both 'live' and filmed interviews. The reporter has two different things to watch: the subject-matter of the interview and the atmosphere in which it is conducted. As to the first, the elementary rule is thorough preparation, and then more preparation. In almost every interview I have done in which the questions or answers have been dull or obscure, it has been so because I could not give enough time to preparation. There is no substitute for this. Only a sound grasp of the subject can enable the interviewer to pick out essential points with sureness and clarity. He must concentrate on essentials because interviews must be contained within very restricted time-limits. He cannot beat about the bush. Even long interviews are succinct exchanges compared with ordinary conversation.

It is easy enough to sling vague wide-ranging questions, after a quick glance at a few press cuttings. This will merely produce vague wide-ranging answers in return. Worse still, it may earn the interviewer a sharp rebuke for inaccurate generalization, or a request for greater clarity in the question. I can never understand why more people, especially eminent ones, do not hit back at incompetent interviewers, or even competent ones. If he has not done his homework or clarified his thoughts the interviewer deserves to be slapped down. The cause of robust interviewing has been done a disservice by questioners who want to imitate the so-called 'tough' style but don't bother to do their homework. This makes them look foolish and clumsy. It also makes it hard to persuade the person interviewed to appear again. People who have been crudely or unfairly questioned on TV remember it for a long time. I don't blame them.

The interviewer should know enough about the person being questioned to anticipate any answer. For an important interview on a big issue it is a good idea to have several follow-up questions ready after every main one to meet any foreseeable answer. But the interviewer should not expect to rely entirely on prepared questions. He cannot cover every eventuality. Nor is it in the least desirable that he should. While keeping his eye on the points he wants to raise, he must be ready for surprises. Without thorough preparation he cannot cope with the surprise answer effectively. He must follow the answers closely. In other words, he must listen. There are too many interviews in which this does not happen. Apart from any question of efficiency, it is elementary politeness. One of the worst faults of interviewing is to ignore an answer by following it with a prepared question, without any relevance to the answer it follows. (This is particularly noticeable in programmes where the interviewer is merely a producer's parrot, relying on someone else's research and someone else's brains, and is incapable of following up an unexpected answer.) Every interviewer is guilty of this fault on occasions, especially when he is pressed for time and sees the frantic signals out of the corner of his eye. But it should be part of his skill to listen to an answer, phrase the next question, note the time-signals, work out how many questions he has room for—and decide which they shall be—all at the same time. It is not easy, but it comes.

There is a warning to be given. The interviewer's mind should not be clogged with specialized knowledge. I am liable to get so deeply involved in a subject that I want to raise all manner of ingenious points. It seems a pity to waste them after all the work! The temptation must be resisted. The interview is not an exercise to prove the interviewer's cleverness or industry. It is to assist several million viewers, a large number of whom may never have heard of the person being interviewed or the place where the interview is being done. The good television reporter should see himself as the representative of the ordinary viewer. *He should not overestimate the viewer's interest, but he should not underestimate his intelligence.*

The television interviewer's technique of questioning has to be different from a newspaperman's—though the object is the same. The former editor of ITN, Sir Geoffrey Cox, with many years of Fleet Street experience, sums up the two techniques:

'The best writing journalist will often take plenty of time stalking around his subject, taking up minor points before he comes to his main question, noting a fact here, or an emphasis there, and then sifting out his material later when he sits down at the typewriter.

But the television journalist is forced to go to the point at once, as bluntly and curtly as is practicable. . . .

His questions must also be designed to produce compact answers. In this sense he has to be sub-editing his final story as he goes along, for though film can be cut, it cannot be compressed. What is more, the TV interviewer must be able to think quickly on his own feet, so as to be able to take up any point in an answer which, left alone, might be obscure or might give bias to the programme.'

No less important than the content of the interview is the tone and atmosphere. The interviewer must see that he grips the attention of the person interviewed. He should be both stimulator and distractor. He must stimulate people to be their natural selves in unnatural surroundings. He must distract them from the cameras, cameramen, lights, microphones, wires, and cables which accompany a TV interview. This applies to both 'live' and filmed interviewing. In the studio the person interviewed must be so encouraged, or provoked, as to forget all the artificial surroundings which stand between him and the audience at home. In a filmed interview done in a person's home or office the setting is less artificial with technical paraphernalia on a smaller scale. But there is more of a 'staged' feeling than there is in the studio. There

is no immediate, warming sense of audience. The interview may not
be seen for several days. In distance, and in time, you are remote from
the viewers. You are working 'cold'.

Even more than in the studio it is important in filmed interviews that
the television reporter should 'defrost' the person interviewed. Stiffness
and self-consciousness may be aggravated by the presence of a small
audienc on the spot—officials, relatives, or passers-by who have
gathered to watch the filming. What does the interviewer do? It
depends who he is interviewing. If the person is diffident or tongue-
tied, questions should be friendly and sympathetic, and if possible
humorous. The moment of a smile is often the first moment that a
person comes to life on the screen. If the person questioned is a self-
possessed, controlled individual, then the questions may have to be
provocative to make him 'give'. President Kennedy, for instance,
when I interviewed him at the time he was campaigning for the Democratic nomination, gave somewhat mechanical answers to questions
about his political record. It was only by pressing two or three times a
question which he had not answered very adequately, about his attitude to McCarthyism, that the tough character of this casually spoken
man emerged. 'Do you now agree that McCarthyism was an evil
thing?' I persisted. 'Perhaps you would let me use my own words,'
he snapped. A passing moment and a simple enough thing for a
Senator to say to a television interviewer, but it caught that glint in his
eye and that jut of his chin which we were to know so well in the
Presidential campaign. It did not disconcert him, nor was he angry, but
it gave a revealing flash of the steel in him.

The interviewer's questions are only one way to enliven proceedings.
The mobility of 16 mm film cameras offers another. This is to film in a
natural setting, away from the office desks and garden chairs. The trouble
is that the natural setting of many of those who have to be interviewed
is an office desk or a garden chair. It is rarely possible to persuade a
busy Prime Minister or Governor to be interviewed in a more active
situation. A farmer can be interviewed on his tractor, an engine-
driver in his locomotive, a pilot in his cockpit. I interviewed Senator
Hubert Humphrey as he was travelling from one engagement to
another on the miniature underground railway between the Capitol and
the Senate Office building. It was in fact the only place and time I could
get a word with this dynamic Senator. This made a welcome change

from the desk interview against a Capitol backcloth in the Senate TV studio. It caught the incredible hustle and rush of a Senator's life.

Enthusiasm for a natural setting should not go too far. Sometimes simplicity gives the best result. A man's face and voice are often all that matter. The background should be there—but only to set the scene, not to dominate it. It is preferable that what is said in the interview is not completely obscured by movement, noise, wind, or rain.

VOX POP

A familiar technique of film reporting is the random 'street' interview with anonymous passers-by. The word 'street' is merely a convenient tag. These interviews are done in all sorts of places—factories, markets, fairgrounds, meetings. This has become a television cliché. It has been used too often as a lazy and convenient method of covering almost any story. Interviews with the man in the street have been shown on every conceivable occasion. They have been used for annual events like the Budget or Christmas, and for big events like an American election. Innumerable passers-by on the streets of the world's capital cities have been buttonholed by inquisitive television reporters on every subject from sex to H-bombs. The United States has been a favourite source of these interviews. The American man (and woman!) in the street has proved a bottomless well of comment on any topic at any time. It is a pity that this has been overdone, because used in the right way 'street' interviews can be superb television journalism. As well as being vastly entertaining, they are an extremely useful method of reporting.

Of what value are the snap comments of uninformed people on complex political issues? I dislike the implications of this objection. You might as well ask why such people should be allowed to vote. But on journalistic grounds alone, these random interviews can be valuable in several ways. Their spontaneous comments can sum up widely held opinions in clear, down-to-earth language. At a big moment they can catch the mood of ordinary people—bitter, excited, overjoyed, bewildered. They can show whether any clear or informed public opinion exists on a particular issue. For instance, it might be instructive to interview people in the street on the question: 'Do you think Britain should join the Common Market?' The answers might not add to our knowledge about the Common Market, but they would show

how little this critical issue is comprehended. This in itself may be revealing, alarming, or even hilarious. Random interviews can illustrate abstract issues in personal terms. They are a reminder that no political or economic problem has any meaning except in terms of people. By all means let us see and hear the men responsible—the politicians and the experts, but let us also see those whose servants they are, the people.

How should these man-in-the-street interviews be used? They are most valuable when the topic is very close to the personal lives of the people questioned; or so big as to command the interest of the ordinary citizen or a social question that has personal meaning for most people. A large number of interviews should always be shot—about seven or eight times as many as are to be used—so that a good cross-section of views and people can be selected. In the case of news which has suddenly burst on the public, and on which no divisions of opinion are yet known, 'street' interviews should only be used for the express purpose of showing random reactions. It should not be pretended that the selection of opinions proves anything. It is television's equivalent of the newspaperman's 'A waitress said . . . The policeman commented . . .' The comments are touches of colour and humanity to record the impact of a big event.

Where there is a big issue with a clash of opinion it is legitimate to use 'street' interviews to define the opposing opinions. Here especially it is important to shoot a great many interviews, continuing until you have filmed as wide a variety of people as possible. The interviews must by carefully selected to reflect opposing views. In other words, the 'random' interviews will not be 'random' when they get to your screen. A choice will have been made from those which come out well on film. The producer will base his selection on all the research which has gone into the programme—including the reporter's own inquiries on the spot, which go far beyond those which the viewer sees on film.

DOMINUS ROBINUS DAY

On one memorable occasion I had a letter of introduction in Latin. This was in the hope of interviewing a Cardinal, leader of the Roman Catholic Church in an Iron Curtain country. The introduction was from a Catholic bishop[1] in Britain whom I had recently interviewed. He was very television-minded, extremely helpful, and we got on well together. The more critical the questions the more he had enjoyed it. His letter was written in Latin because he and the Cardinal had no other common language. Here is how the jet-age television man was heralded in the language of centuries past:

'*Eminentissime Princeps,*

Dominus Robinus Day, qui a mea manu has praesentes litteras accepit nomine haud ignoto fruitur in medio communicationis quod vulgo "television" nuncupatur.

Cum pluribus diversarum nationum egregiis personis per televisionem est jam collocatus, nunc autem enixe rogat eandem collequendi facultatem benigne ut ei concedire digneris.

Idem D. Day licet acatholicus vir est optimae famae. . . .'

For the television reporter's convenience, a translation was attached:

'Your Eminence,

Mr Robin Day, who has received this letter from my hands, enjoys a reputation in the field of communications commonly known as "television".

He has already had television interviews with a number of well-known people in many countries. He now begs your Eminence to deign to give him the same opportunity of an interview.

Mr Day is not a Catholic but he is a man of excellent reputation. . . .'

As I feared, this impressive document did not secure an interview, so delicate and dangerous was the Cardinal's position, but it did enable us to film one of his rare public appearances.

CUTS AND CUT-AWAYS

It sometimes happens that people complain about the way their interview has been cut. People likewise complain that newspapers have not reported them fairly. These are questions of editorial judgment and

---

[1]Later to become His Eminence Cardinal John Heenan.

integrity. So far as television film is concerned, editing presents certain difficulties which do not affect a newspaper. In the printed report, a sentence here or a word there can be omitted to leave only the important points without altering the meaning. You can summarize and compress. With film you can only cut. A newspaper can pick out a vital phrase from the middle of a long passage. On film this may be impossible, because of the tone of voice and the flow of words. You may have to use all or none of the passage concerned. This emphasizes the need for questions which define and limit the area of the answers. One way of dealing with a long answer (but only if its sense permits it to be broken down conveniently) is to cut in close shots of the interviewer listening, or long shots of the interview scene, between the extracts selected. This can look jerky, and shortage of time may make it hard to choose the most suitable shot of the interviewer. He should not be shown grinning broadly in the middle of a deadly serious answer, nor nodding his agreement to a monstrous falsehood.

A similar method is used to link extracts from speeches. Between chosen sentences are interpolated shots of the audience listening or applauding. Here again care must be taken in choosing the shot. Embarrassing mistakes can occur in the hectic rush to get film edited and on the air. In an early TV report of a Labour Party Conference, a 'cut-away' shot inserted between extracts of a speech showed Mr Harold Wilson applauding vigorously. This was fine, except that the speaker he was shown to be applauding was Mr Harold Wilson.

SIMPLY A MEANS OF SEEING

I have mentioned some of the professional techniques which television journalism demands. They are not everything. It is much too easy to get obsessed with technique and presentation, with smoothness and 'effect'. In the long run the only thing that matters is the value of what appears on that small screen for someone sitting in a room in Bermondsey or Bradford. Is it clear? Is it true? Is it real? All the production technique and professional skill of everyone concerned are wasted if the product is obscure, phoney, artificial. Too much cleverness and pre-arrangement can often bring these results. Television is not an end in itself. Its most memorable moments are when the screen, in Bernard

Levin's phrase, 'looks in on life and comes alive'. If television is an art at all, it is the art of no art, the art of reality.

I shall never forget an interview with a woman guide at Auschwitz concentration camp in southern Poland. The vast area of Auschwitz is still preserved as a monument to Nazi atrocity. The ruined gas-chambers and crematoria are seen by thousands of visitors. The woman guide had been an inmate of Auschwitz. She conducted us round the camp without any trace of emotion. In calm matter-of-fact tones she pointed out the crematoria, the gas-chambers, the railway that brought 4 million people to their deaths, and the execution yard where 25,000 political prisoners had been shot. She took us through the museum with the rooms piled full of human hair, and, most horrible of all, little children's shoes. She showed us the rows of wooden huts where the forced-labour squads had lived. Some have been cleaned out and are on exhibition for visitors to see. I asked her where she had lived. We drove with her to another part of the camp, which is so huge that some of the huts are left in the same condition as they were when the camp was liberated. They were not part of the normal visitor's tour.

She led us to her own hut. It was still (this was in 1959) a filthy shambles with rusty soup-bowls and tin cans lying about the floor. 'Where did you sleep?' I asked. As the cameraman filmed, she pointed to the wooden shelf ten feet wide where she and five other women had slept side by side for four years. I asked if she would allow me to interview her there and then. She willingly agreed. In a few minutes the cameraman and recordist had set up their sound equipment outside the hut and were filming through a window. The woman told how she had been arrested at the age of seventeen in 1940 and spent the next five years in concentration camps. As she spoke, she ceased to be an Auschwitz guide. She became an Auschwitz inmate standing on the very spot where she had lived through hell. 'Why,' I asked, and I could scarcely bear to put the question, 'why do you stay here working as a guide fifteen years after the end of it all?' Until then she had kept control of herself. Now her voice faltered and tears came into her eyes. 'So that people can see that these things will never happen again.' In that single moment was all the anguish of a broken life.

Our young Polish interpreter translated her answer softly, his voice trembling. But somehow one knew what she had said. Standing there in that sickening place, listening to that woman, the problems of our own lives seemed shamefully trivial. It was profoundly moving to us, not least for the cameraman, George Richardson, a tough professional who had seen some grim things in his time. The emotion caught him even as he handled the camera. He closed in instinctively, following the woman's story, till at the end that face which told a terrible story filled the picture. No sooner had we finished than I wondered if we had done wrong in filming her in that state of emotion, I asked her whether she minded if we used film of her being so upset. No, she did not mind at all. My mind was eased by the words she had used: 'So that people can see that these things will never happen again.'

A few days later I watched the reactions of those who saw this interview transmitted. We showed every foot of the film. Girls who were babes in arms when that woman was an Auschwitz prisoner stopped their chattering and typing. They were visibly affected. Yet this was not a good piece of television 'production'. It was unpremeditated, unplanned, unrehearsed, undirected. I had done nothing except ask what I felt moved to ask. The woman had done nothing except say what she felt moved to say. The cameraman had done nothing except focus his lens on her face. No technique, no art—nothing—came between that woman and the viewers who watched her. It was not a piece of television, it was a piece of humanity. Television simply happened to be there, not as an art or a technique, but as a means of seeing.

Index